Sibylle Hechtel

# FUN CLIMBS
# COLORADO
## Best Family Climbing Vacations

## Sharp End Publishing
Authentic Guides From Core Climbers

## FUN CLIMBS COLORADO:
### BEST CLIMBING VACATIONS FOR FRIENDS AND FAMILY by Sibylle Hechtel

Published and distributed by:
Sharp End Publishing LLC
PO Box 1613
Boulder, CO 80306
p. 303.444.2698
www.sharpendbooks.com

ISBN: 978-1-892540-51-5

**Cover Photo Credits:** Kira Paik (left) and Jaclyn Paik on **Gina's Surprise** 5.4, and Tristan Hechtel on **Wind Ridge** 5.6.

**Opening Page Photo Credit**: Jaclyn Paik on **Gina's Surprise** 5.4.

A kick ass job by Steve "Crusher" Bartlett for maps.
All unlabeled photos are credited to the author Sibylle Hechtel.

# READ THIS BEFORE USING THIS BOOK
# WARNING:

Climbing is a very dangerous activity. Take all precautions and evaluate your ability carefully. Use judgment rather than the opinions represented in this book. The publisher and author assume no responsibility for injury or death resulting from the use of this book. This book is based on opinions. Do not rely on information, descriptions, or difficulty ratings as these are entirely subjective. If you are unwilling to assume complete responsibility for your safety, do not use this guidebook.

THE AUTHOR AND PUBLISHER EXPRESSLY DISCLAIM ALL REPRESENTATIONS AND WARRANTIES REGARDING THIS GUIDE, THE ACCURACY OF THE INFORMATION HEREIN, AND THE RESULTS OF YOUR USE HEREOF, INCLUDING WITHOUT LIMITATION, IMPLIED WARRANTIES OF MERCHANTABILITY AND FITNESS FOR A PARTICULAR PURPOSE. THE USER ASSUMES ALL RISK ASSOCIATED WITH THE USE OF THIS GUIDE.

It is your responsibility to take care of yourself while climbing. Seek a professional instructor or guide if you are unsure of your ability to handle any circumstances that may arise. This guide is not intended as an instructional manual.

## Dedication

This book is dedicated to my father Richard Hechtel and my mother Lisa Hechtel, who taught me how to climb, and to my son Tristan Hechtel, who makes climbing even more fun.

## Acknowledgements

I want to thank all of the people who helped me with this book. First I'd like to thank Fred and Heidi Knapp for their support and encouragement, and for reading through early drafts to provide feedback on where the book should go from there. I also want to thank all of the many people who climbed easy routes on their climbing trip so that I could take pictures of them, and friends who took their children climbing somewhere that I wanted to take pictures.

Last, but not least, I want to thank my son Tristan who climbed nearly every one of the more than 120 routes in the book so that I could take pictures from above, from below, sideways, and get background scenery. He spent hours leading climbs and then holding me on belay while I pendulumed back and forth to take pictures.

### A Special Thanks To:

| | | | | | |
|---|---|---|---|---|---|
| Brian | Adelman | Amy | Fluet | Anne | Rees |
| Isabella | Adelman | Charlie | Gray | Lizzy | Scully |
| Johan | Adelman | Sallie | Greenwood | Lauren | Sigman |
| Madeleine | Adelman | Dan | McDonnell | Stan | Spencer |
| Beth | Bennett | Corinne | McKay | Rick | Thompson |
| Roger | Briggs | Gabriel | Metzger | Cindy | Trotter |
| Greg | Brown | Leo | Paik | Mary | Turner |
| Tarrie | Burnett | Jaclyn | Paik | Dan | Urist |
| Chad | Davis | Kira | Paik | Ada | Urist |
| Eric | Doub | Erin | Paik | Thomas | Walsh |
| Randy | Emmons | Tom | Perkins | Sarah | Watson |
| Megan | Emmons | Ernie | Port | Mike | Wolfson |
| John | Farmer | Dana | Prosser | Noemi | from France |

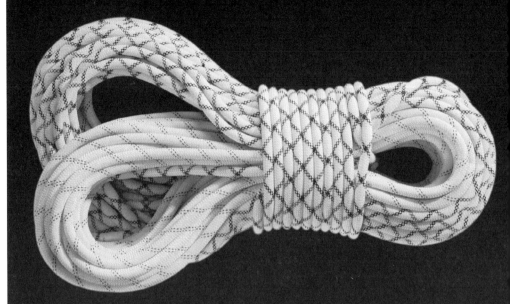

# THE RIGHT ROPE

Daunting exposure, desperate redpoints, punishing off-widths, delicate verglas – no worries, with your new Sterling, you have the right rope. Sterling spent many climbing seasons developing a whole new line of dynamic climbing ropes and improving our trademark DryCore™. The result: the right rope for your next climbing adventure. Our new Marathon™ line has the same ultra durable sheath, but a more supple hand. Our Evolution™ line has been redesigned for high performance: lighter with lower impact forces, for those grueling redpoints, committing alpine lines, or trad routes. When faced with endless amounts of fixing, hauling, and rapping, consider our workhorse static lines–the SuperStatic™ and HTP Static™. Whatever corner of the world you're going to, take the right rope.

**MARATHON. EVOLUTION. NITRO. SUPERSTATIC. HTP STATIC.**
The right ropes for all your climbing endeavors.

**STERLING ROPE**

**Engineered. Tested. Proven.**

**WWW.STERLINGROPE.COM**

# TABLE OF CONTENTS

# PUBLISHER'S NOTE

### The Group Leader
This guide makes an assumption of a competent, responsible group leader. This individual must have the experience and temperament to plan for whatever variables may arise, be it a tired, hungry or hurt kid, inclement weather, and any number of routefinding and anchor placement difficulties. If there is no one in the group that fits this description, hire a guide or stay in the climbing gym. It's that simple.

### Route Grades..."This feels hard!"
This book should not be treated as an extension of the climbing gym. If you've been climbing in the gym, be sure to subtract a number grade or two when determining how hard you're "really" climbing. As the leader, be super comfortable at the grade you chose to climb. As a mention, most of the areas in this book are a bit old school in regard to their ratings, meaning the climbs may seem stout for the grade. If you're feeling sandbagged, reset your internal route-o-meter to 1990, or maybe even 1985. You'll have more fun, and you'll stop cursing the writer for getting you on something hard. If you want a more casual experience (no multi-pitch climbing, no long hikes) put *Front Range Topropes* by Fred Knapp in your climbing pack as a back-up plan.

### Plan, Plan, Plan (add the word "plan" for each kid you bring)
Study this guide in advance of your planned trip. In fact, use this guide to plan out your itinerary. You may find that the scope of the guide is limiting and that you need to bring a more comprehensive book for the area you're going to visit. The aim of this guide is to give an overview of the best climbs and climbing areas around Colorado suitable for kids and perhaps older climbers. The determinations were mostly weighed on approach, rock quality, difficulty of the routes, and of course the fun factor.

### Kids and Climbing ("...but my kid climbed 5.11 when he was 10...and hiked to the top of Longs Peak...)
Kids span the rainbow in terms of ability, attitude, and judgement. Only you know the special mix that you're dealing with. One kid's best day ever is another's incessant whine fest. Keep this in mind when reading about any particular climb and its demands. Some kids just don't have patience, calmness, listening skills, or endurance to be in a climbing environment. Some are born knowing not to throw rocks, not to stand in the plumb line of a cliff top, and not to jump about like a Jedi in training. Tristan, the son of the author, was one of these exceptional kids. He's also grown up into a high schooler taking nearly every AP class offered, including the physics class I dropped out of in college.

### A Little Climbing, A Little Playing
This guide does an exceptionally good job of helping plan a balanced trip. There's just enough good climbing to steer you in the right direction combined with other fun nearby outings.

### Feedback
We're sure future editions will benefit from your experiences. Please write Sibylle Hechtel at sibylle@nasw.org.

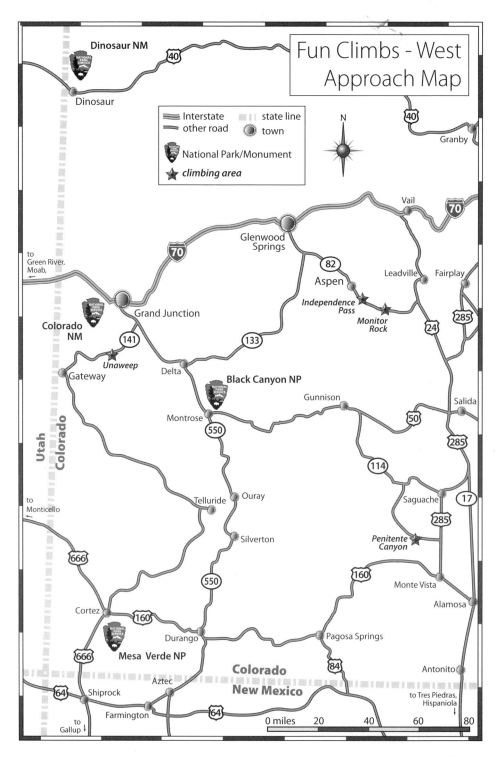

Fun Climbs - West
Approach Map

Interstate
other road
state line
town
National Park/Monument
*climbing area*

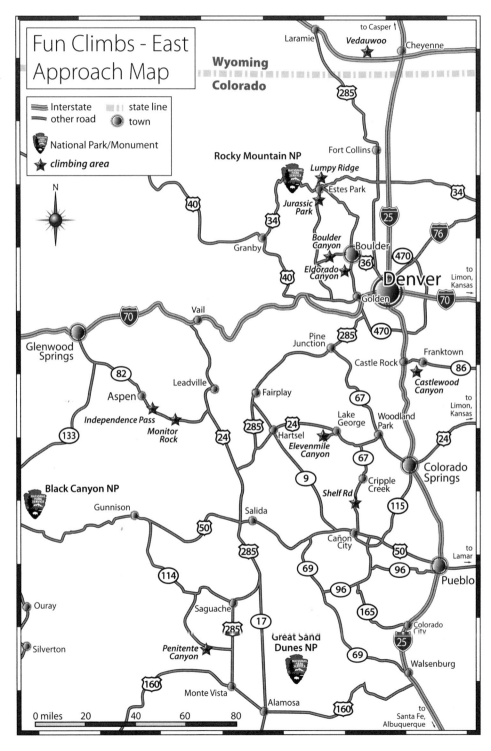

# Fun Climbs - East Approach Map

**Legend:**
- ≡ Interstate
- — other road
- ▮▮ state line
- ◉ town
- National Park/Monument
- ★ *climbing area*

N

**Wyoming / Colorado**

to Casper ↑

Laramie
*Vedauwoo* ★
Cheyenne

285

Fort Collins

Rocky Mountain NP
*Lumpy Ridge* ★
Estes Park
34

*Jurassic Park* ★

40
34

Granby

*Boulder Canyon* ★
Boulder
36
470
76

*Eldorado Canyon* ★
40

**Denver**
Golden
470
70
to Limon, Kansas

Vail
70

Glenwood Springs

Pine Junction
285
470

Castle Rock
Franktown
86
*Castlewood Canyon* ★

82
Leadville

Aspen
Fairplay
67
to Limon, Kansas

*Independence Pass*
*Monitor Rock* ★
133

Lake George
Woodland Park
24

285
24
Hartsel
*Elevenmile Canyon* ★
67

Black Canyon NP
Gunnison

9
Cripple Creek
*Shelf Rd* ★
115

Colorado Springs

50
Salida

285
Cañon City
50
to Lamar

114

69
96
Pueblo

Ouray

Saguache
17
165

Silverton
285
*Penitente Canyon* ★

Great Sand Dunes NP
69
Colorado City
25
Walsenburg

160
Monte Vista
Alamosa
160
to Santa Fe, Albuquerque ↘

0 miles    20    40    60    80

9

*Fun Climbs Colorado* will jump start your rock climbing vacation. Whether you're a Colorado native trying to organize a weekend adventure with the kids or a vacationing climber out with your family, I hope to direct you to the best places and routes for your excursion.

I wrote this book for families on a climbing vacation or climbers on their first road trip. I want to advise climbers who take their small children along to the base of climbs, or take older kids and teach them to climb; for climbers who want to take their parents, grandparents, or other relatives climbing, and for everyone who wants to share their joy in climbing with inexperienced or handicapped friends. Check here not only for climbs and climbing areas that are easily accessible, but also for information about nearby camping, lodging, restaurants, stores and other logistical information such as extra things to take, equipment for kids, and special precautions.

I'll discuss the rock quality, the quality of the routes, the approaches and descents, the availability of bolts in sport climbs, and the ease of gear placements in crack climbs, as well as mention possible dangers (such as rattlesnakes, scorpions or cactus spines).

Last, kids like climbing trips to areas that offer many fun things to do, like hot springs, horseback rides, and white water rafting. A section titled "What Else Can We Do That's Fun?" covers local attractions for rest day or after-climbing activities.

As a child, climbing with my dad, Dr. Richard Hechtel in Germany

Climbing with my dad in the 70s in Tuolomne.

This guide is the culmination of experience gained growing up in a climbing environment as well as traveling with my son over the past 15 years. From age three, my German parents toted me (along with my grandmother) to climbs in the German Alps, France, Italy and Switzerland, and after we immigrated to destinations throughout the United States. I found myself in Yosemite's famous Camp 4 when I was just 10 or 11. It was only natural that when my son, Tristan, came along he'd be a part of this climbing heritage as well. Early on I'd meet my parents in Idaho's City of Rocks, Hueco Tanks, Texas, or Yosemite where I'd climb with my father while my mother played with Tristan. We needed a place where my father could still do the approach, and my mother was comfortable playing with a very active toddler.

Over the years I've met many families doing similar trips as I did with Tristan. In October 2005, I met a California couple whose Midwest parents had rendezvoused with them in Indian Creek, Utah to care for their grandchild as well as enjoy the amazing scenery. Repeated encounters, like this one, provided the inspiration for this project.

Kids grow amazingly fast and will improve more quickly than you expect. At age seven, my son climbed 5.10 cracks on toprope, at 8 he could follow some 5.11s, and when he was 11 years old, he started leading me up routes. I've met children who have lead 5.12 or harder by age 12. If you put in a little time and effort, you can raise a rope gun for when you become old and decrepit. Of course by then you'll be watching a 4-year-old grandchild at the base hoping to get a ride on a few pitches.

Enjoy!

First lead! Is that dog's head Pluto?

## ABOUT THIS BOOK

### Who this book is for:

This book is for experienced climbers who know how to climb, place gear and find themselves in the position of trip leader for kids, parents, or friends. Perhaps they live in Colorado but have never had to consider all the variables of climbing with kids, or maybe the leader has climbed very little or not at all in Colorado. It could be you're bringing your friends or family on their first climbing trip out west. If you're from Yosemite or the East, your parents live in Iowa, and you're meeting in Colorado to climb while grandma minds the toddler, this book can recommend the best places to go. I'll describe which climbing areas are most suitable for your friends and family and which climbs at these areas would provide the most pleasure (or the least difficulty).

### Who it is not for:

This book is not to help people teach themselves how to climb, place anchors, or how to belay. I assume you have mastered all these skills, and more, before taking your friends and family out to climb. I don't intend to teach novice climbers or non-climbers with little or no previous experience. If you've only climbed a few times, loved it, and want to go with your friends, I will recommend guide schools that can teach you to climb safely.

## CHOICES, CHOICES, CHOICES

### I've selected certain climbs in Colorado provided they have:

• A relatively short, easy approach
• A safe, easy descent
• The climb is relatively easy, on good quality rock, with enjoyable movement, and few or no objective dangers
• The base area is relatively flat, safe, free of objective hazards (rockfall, poison ivy, exposure to cliffs, cacti)
• The climb is well-protected, either with good, well-spaced bolts or easily placed gear

### I've included climbing areas if they have:

• Several quality climbs that meet the above criteria
• Good camping nearby (if possible)
• Pleasant scenery, beautiful, nice atmosphere
• Fun activities nearby
• Safe climbs, rock, base areas

Penitente provides great "caves" for Batman and Spider-Man

## HOW TO USE THIS BOOK

Thumbs Up &
Thumbs Down

Area
Characteristics

Hike Time

Rock Type

Gear

Kid Age

Camping

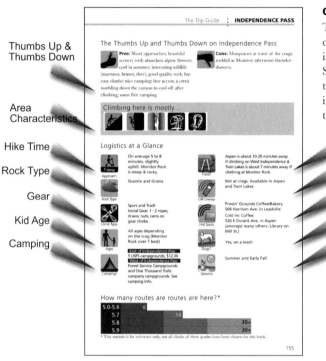

**Opening Spread**

This spread begins each chapter, giving vital information at a glance. Some of this information is expounded on in the ensuing pages of the chapters.

Food Available

Cell Phone Coverage

Internet Access

Dogs Allowed?

Best Seasons

## The Trip Guide

### Specifics on Logistics

GETTING THERE

Directions to the climbing area.

SETTING UP
CAMP

HOTELS &
MOTELS

What amenities can you expect at the campgrounds? Do you need reservations or is it first-come first-served?

SHOPPING &
GROCERIES

Description of local grocery stores, health food stores, restaurants, and cafes.

RESTAURANTS
& COFFEE

Recommended and/or nearby eating establishments.

### What Else Can We Do That's Fun?

BOULDERING

MOUNTAIN
BIKING

HIKING

REST DAY
ACTIVITIES

This guide describes fun things to do on rest days, nearby excursions to exciting places, and neat places to shop. The options may include bouldering, hiking, mountain biking, rafting, nearby climbing gyms for a rainy day, horseback riding, amusement parks, local attractions, mini golf, museums, zoos, rodeos, bison ranches, wolf sanctuaries, nearby National Monuments and Preserves, wildlife refuges, and last but not least, shopping!

This guide highlights a few of any area's high-quality easier climbs. If you like a place enough that you want to stay a week or longer, you could buy the guide to that area.

The Trip Guide ⋮ **INDEPENDENCE PASS**

**REST DAY ACTIVITIES**

**Aspen Center for Environmental Studies**
ACES at Hallam Lake, 100 Puppy Smith St., Aspen
(970) 925.5756    aces@aspennature.org

**Rock Bottom Ranch**
2001 Hooks Spur Road, Basalt, CO 81621
(970) 927.6760    rockbottom@sopris.net
This environmental education center has two locations - the 25-acre Hallam Lake Nature Preserve and a 113-acre Wildlife Preserve at Rock Bottom Ranch in Basalt. Hallam Lake features a self-guided nature trail with meadows, a pond, marsh, and many birds.

Other Guides

**OTHER CLIMBING GUIDES**

*Independence Pass Rock Climbing*, Tom Perkins, 2003.
This guide covers both climbing and bouldering along Independence Pass. Purchase of the guidebook confers access to new route information on their website.    www.aspenclimbingguides.com
*Rock Climbing Colorado*, Stewart Green, 1995.
*Colorado Bouldering*, Phillip Benningfield, 2005
*Colorado Bouldering 2*, Phillip Benningfield, 2003

Important Numbers

**EMERGENCY INFORMATION & MORE**

**Hospitals**
**St Vincent Hospital**
822 W 4th St, Leadville
(719) 486-0250

**Heart of the Rockies Medical**
448 E 1st St, Salida
(719) 539-6661

**St Vincent General Hospital**
400 Washington St, Leadville
(719) 486-1504

**Aspen Valley Hospital**
401 Castle Creek Rd, Aspen
(970) 925-1120

**Rangers**
**Leadville Ranger District**
2015 North Poplar
Leadville, CO 80461
(719) 486-0749

**Aspen Ranger District**
806 West Hallam
Aspen, CO 81611
(970) 925-3445

**Guide Schools**
**Aspen Expeditions**
426 S. Spring St.
Aspen, CO
(970) 925-7625
aspenexpeditions.com

To hire a guide in the Aspen area, try Aspen Expeditions (an AMGA certified service), which offers guided rock climbing, mountaineering, and high altitude trekking. A private guide will cater to any group size, age or experience level.

165

Naptime

15

## ICONS

Icons at the beginning of each area will help familiarize you with the essential information at a glance. If you're looking for slab climbs with PM sun and a five minute hike, this is your quick reference

### Approach Information and Time

Easy    Moderate    Difficult

### Direction Cliff Faces (AKA Are you in the sun?)

North    South    EAST    WEST

### Rock Steepness

Slab    Vertical    Steep    Roof

### Climbing Type

Mixed    Sport    Traditional
Trad Gear/    Gear    Gear
Quickdraws

### Nature of the Climbing

Crimpy    Powerful    Pumpy    Technical    Crack    Pockets    Cobbles    Offwidth

### Descent Information

Rappel Required    Walk

### Warning

Tyrolean    Wade

## STAR RATINGS

**0 STARS:** Not that great, included for completeness
★ **STARS:** Good route
★★ **STARS:** Very good route, lots of fun
★★★ **STARS:** Terrific route, must do
★★★★ **STARS:** Absolutely fantastic climb, worth doing several times

## BASIC CLIMBING STUFF

• Ropes, rope bag
• Rack, runners
• Shoes, harness, helmet, chalk bag
• Web-o-lette, daisy chain
• Guidebooks
• Stick clip
• Knee pads
• Crash pad
• Camelback

## THE STANDARD GEAR RACK

RPs - about 3-4 medium size
wired stoppers: about 4-6 small
slung stoppers (on perlon), med to lg stoppers
Cams: Camalot: 0.5, 0.75, 1, 2
TCUs: # 2,3,4

"Besides food and water, our essentials include spare biners, clothesline or other thin, packable rope and a maimed GI-Joe or other action figure. Nate can amaze himself for a remarkable length of time by tying Joe to trees, flinging his bound body from cliffs and sliding him down zip-lines, preferably into things that leave marks." -Heather Perrin

## A FEW CAMPING SUGGESTIONS

| Camping stuff | Bath, etc. | Food & Prep |
|---|---|---|
| Tent | Towel | Stove, fuel, dish soap, pots, frying pan, |
| Tarp | Toiletries | spatula, bowls, utensils. |
| Parachute cord | Shampoo | Gatorade, dry milk, hot chocolate, |
| Sleeping bag | Swiss army knife | olive oil, soy sauce, gorp, cereal, instant |
| Pad | TP | oats, bars, bread, bagels, cheese, tuna, |
| Headlamp | Sewing kit | soups. |
| Maps | Camera | Burritos: onions, dried beans, cheese, |
| Water bottles | Batteries | tortillas, spices. |
| | | Zip lock baggies. |

## KIDS AND COMPLAINING....PLAN AHEAD FOR THE CLIMBING PACK

**The major categories:** Hungry, Thirsty, Tired, Cold, Hot, Wet, Bored, Sick, Hurt. Know your kid and plan accordingly. Below are a few considerations. This list is not complete and you'll certainly want to add to it.

Water & Food:.....................................
Many of the areas in the guide don't have water at the base or trailhead. Buy plenty and possibly bring a filter.
• Water bottles/Hydration pack
• Filter
• Snacks (healthy and unhealthy), sandwiches, energy bars

Safety & First Aid Kit:..............................
• Helmet (for kids at the base too)
• Tweezers & Needle
• Band Aids/Butterfly bandage
• Gauze and Compress cloth
• Advil or painkillers both for kids and adults

The Sun:.............................................
• Sunscreen & chapstick
• Brimmed Hat/Visor
• Sunglasses

Clothing:............................................
• Rain gear
• Sandals and/or extra shoes
• Windbreaker, Pile Jacket/Pants
• Shorts, T-Shirt
• Gloves, Hat

Climbing Basics for Kids:.........................
• Harness
• Climbing Shoes
• Chalk Bag
• Helmet

Keeping Busy at the Base:.......................
Depending on the ages of kids, some of the following could be helpful in your pack.
• Crayons, Markers, Paper, Workbooks, Books
• Action Figures, Cards
• Bucket & Shovels
• A Crazy Creek chair (sitting and naps)
• Gameboy or other electronic game

Waste:.............................................
• Trowel for catholes
• TP & lighter
• Wagbag for carryout in sensitive areas
• Moist towels, Ziplocks
• Diapers, wipes, diaper bag

"The most important thing to bring to the cliff if you're bringing a child is another child." -Lynn Hill

## AREAS IN GUIDE COMPARED
## STAR RATING CHART

| AREA NAME | CLIMBING | CAMPING | ACTIVITIES | SAFETY |
|---|---|---|---|---|
| Vedauwoo | ★★ | ★★★ | ★★ | ★★ |
| Estes Park | ★★★ | ★★ | ★★★ | ★★ |
| Boulder Area | ★★★ | 0 | ★★★ | ★ |
| Castlewood Canyon | ★ | 0 | ★★ | ★★ |
| Elevenmile & The South Platte | ★★ | ★★★ | ★ | ★★ |
| Shelf Road | ★★★ | ★★★ | ★★★ | ★★★ |
| Independence Pass | ★★★ | ★★★ | ★★ | ★★ |
| Penitente Canyon | ★★ | ★★★ | ★ | ★★★ |
| Unaweep | ★ | ★★ | ★ | ★ |

The Nautilus, one of the beautiful granite outcrops of Vedauwoo

# VEDAUWOO ( ... WE KNOW THIS IS WYOMING!)

Imagine driving miles across empty prairie when suddenly, about a mile off the freeway, a jumbled pile of rocks appears. This jumble, somewhat reminiscent of Joshua Tree, comprises the Vedauwoo Recreation Area, part of the Medicine Bow National Forest. After turning off the freeway to enter Vedauwoo, what appears hodge-podge from afar are actually cliffs of quality Sherman granite, with both excellent friction routes and many cracks of all sizes (though at times it may seem like they're mostly offwidths).

Vedauwoo has excellent rock, though a bit rough and abrasive in places, with as little or less rockfall than I've seen anywhere. The approaches tend to be fairly short, though sometimes they involve circuitous trails threading among the many house- and apartment-sized boulders surrounding the cliffs. And finally, Vedauwoo contains more easy climbs than any one other area in Colorado or southern Wyoming — which brings us to why I included Vedauwoo, in Wyoming, in a book about Colorado climbs: proximity. It takes about one and a half hours to drive from Boulder to Vedauwoo, even less from Fort Collins, whereas Unaweep lies about four to five hours from the Front Range; Shelf Road takes over three hours from Boulder; and Penitente is even further away. Plus, you can climb at Vedauwoo in summer when it's too hot elsewhere.

In summer, the weather is generally mild with sunny days and pleasant evenings and nights. (It really has to be summer. Don't count on climbing in early June: the first weekend of June 2005, Vedauwoo received 14 inches of snow). Pleasant camping is a bonus here with 28 grassy sites and flat tent spots scattered among trees and meadows. The unique prairie scenery makes this among the prettiest places to camp and climb.

I will discuss climbs on both Walt's Wall and the Fall Wall, which are close to each other, have short approaches, and include several easy climbs. I'll also describe climbs on the Nautilus, one of which, *Cornelius*, is one of the best easy finger cracks I've done anywhere. It has a short approach, but a somewhat longer descent (at least for the leader of the group).

Numerous fun activities can be found in nearby Cheyenne, including several nationally recognized rodeos.

## The Thumbs Up and Thumbs Down on Vedauwoo...........................

 **Pros:** Short approaches; lovely camping; cool in summer; many easy routes, both crack and friction; pretty scenery including spectacular boulders and rock formations; also free camping on BLM land just outside the Vedauwoo Recreation Area.

 **Cons:** Some approaches are steep or bouldery; some climbs start high on ledges that would be unsafe for small children; windy at times; campground may be full on weekends; some traffic noise from nearby I-80.

## Climbing here is mostly...

## Logistics at a Glance ......................................................................

? time
Approach

8-10 minutes

Food?

Laramie, 16 miles west
Cheyenne, 36 miles east

Rock Type

Granite
with great friction

Cell Coverage

Yes, reception at
campground and at
some climbs.

Climb Type

Gear and Mixed

Hot Spots

No wireless internet

Ages

Best for
ages 7 and up

Dogs?

Yes, on leash

Camping?

Pay $10 night, 28
sites or BLM free (no
amenities). See details
in camping section.

Seasons

Summer

## How many routes are here?*

| | | | |
|---|---|---|---|
| 5.0-5.5 | | 30+ | |
| 5.6 | | 30+ | |
| 5.7 | 25+ | | |
| 5.8 | | | 40+ |

* This statistic is for reference only, not all climbs of these grades have been chosen for this book.

**GETTING THERE**

**From Laramie:** Take I-80 east for 16 miles to Exit 329, Vedauwoo Road. Drive Vedauwoo Road for 1.1 miles to the kiosk. Turn left and into the Vedauwoo Recreation Area. After 0.2 miles turn right to enter the campground or continue straight to the picnic area near the base of Walt's Wall.

**From Cheyenne:** Take I-80 west for about 36 miles to Exit 329.

Instead of turning left toward the camping, continue straight on a dirt road for 0.2 miles to free parking below the Nautilus at the start of the trail heading to the Nautilus. Continue down this road to get to free camping on BLM land and to reach Reynold's Hill.

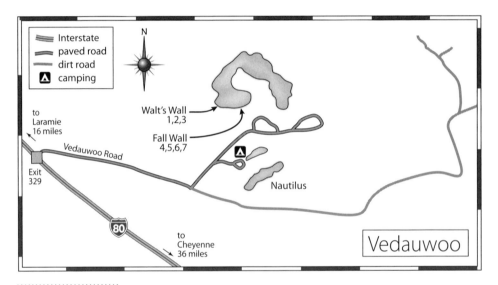

**SETTING UP CAMP**

1. **Vedauwoo proper:** $10.00 per night for a nice level site with water, picnic tables, chemical toilets, and garbage removal. Plus, the camping is close to the climbs. If you register at the campground, you can also park for free at the picnic area near Walt's Wall. Put a note on your dashboard telling the rangers that you are staying in a site in the campground. Camping is currently first-come, first-serve, and with only 28 sites, the campground tends to fill up on weekends.
GPS: 8,057 ft. 13 T 0468356 UTM 4556117

2. **The BLM Option:** Alternatively, camping on BLM land outside the fence is free. There are no amenities, but it's free. The only catch is, it costs $5.00 to park at the picnic area near the base of the Clamshell and Walt's Wall. If you choose to camp on BLM land (or can't get in because all the sites are full), either pay to park near the climbing, or walk further to reach the cliffs.

**MORE
SETTING UP
CAMP**

For other nearby campgrounds that accept reservations, search reserve-USA.com using the keywords *Medicine Bow.*

**HOTELS &
MOTELS**

Along the interstate (I-80 or I-25), you'll see lots of signs for **Little America**, a huge hotel chain. It may not be a five-star hotel but it's cheap, and a good value for what you're paying. After several days camping and climbing, many climbers are ready for a swimming pool and a shower! (307) 775-8400    www.littleamerica.com/cheyenne

**SHOPPING &
GROCERIES**

Head to either Cheyenne or Laramie for groceries and other necessities.

**King Soopers**, 3702 Dell Range Blvd, Cheyenne
(307) 638-0014

**Safeway**, 554 N 3rd St, Laramie
(307) 721-5107

**Medicine Bow Natural Foods**, 119 S 1st St, Laramie (307) 742-2350
This is a new market/deli in downtown Laramie. They have huge omelets with sweet potato hash browns, plate-sized pancakes, sandwiches, a salad bar, smoothies, coffee drinks, kids' meals, deli-style salads, chips and snacks to take along climbing. They use organic ingredients whenever possible.

**Sierra Trading Post**, 5025 Campstool Rd, Cheyenne (307) 775-8090
The Sierra Trading Post, an outdoor clothing outlet store, merits a shopping trip on a rest day. See Rest Day activities for more information.
www.SierraTradingPost.com

Clam Shell

My friend Amy Fluet, who moved from Boulder to Laramie, offers a local's insight into where to eat in Laramie (not a world-renowned gourmet spot). Amy tells me that they "don't have anything super fancy, but these all offer good food." She describes Laramie as a great small town with easy access to the outdoors, affordable housing, little traffic, an old downtown that's not full of fluffy chain stores. What more can you ask?

**Coal Creek Coffee**, 110 East Grand Avenue, (307) 745-7737
A great coffee shop in downtown Laramie that makes their own baked goods. They offer an excellent selection of fresh-baked muffins, pastries (the "pull-aparts" are really good); espresso, chai; salads, panini sandwiches, and breakfast bagels (an egg, cheese and meat sandwich... Amy recommends the prosciutto one).

**Elmer Lovejoy's Bar and Grill**, 101 Grand Ave, (307) 745-0141
Another downtown stop (across the street from Coal Creek Coffee) that offers traditional burgers and fries as well as beer from the local brewpub (same owners), great chocolate milkshakes, burgers, wraps, salads, and a kids' menu. This is a good family-oriented stop, as well as a nice place to have a beer and munchies after climbing (there's a bar in the restaurant).

**Corona Village Andale**, 2900 E Grand Ave, (307) 745-5944
This is a spin off of a good local Mexican restaurant (Corona Village). Corona Andale is on Grand Avenue in a tiny strip mall toward the west end of town. The folks behind the counter work hard and are friendly. The burritos are good and big; I would recommend their specials. They serve beer or margaritas with your meal (as well as soft drinks). They have a good kids' menu, and on Sundays, any item on the kids' menu is less than a buck. Chips (made fresh as you order them) and salsa are free on weekends. No credit cards are accepted, so be sure to take some cash.

**Corona Village**, 421 Boswell Drive, (307) 721-0167
For a more formal dining experience, but still casual and friendly, try Corona Village, near the junction of 287 and I-80. They serve top-shelf margaritas (plan on splitting one with a friend) and they do take credit cards, unlike Corona Andale.

**Sweet Melissas**, 213 South 1st Street, (307) 742-9607
This nice little vegetarian restaurant is also downtown. They have a good selection of sandwiches, lasagna, salads, and a kids' menu.

Edward's Crack 5.7-          Photograph by Richard Hechtel

# What Else Can We Do That's Fun?

## Bouldering

The many oddly shaped boulders strewn around the campground and nearby cliffs provide some spontaneous bouldering opportunities. However, The School Yard area, not a far drive, offers a wide range of V0-V3 problems. If you're coming from Vedauwoo, head west on I-80 to the Happy Jack exit. Go west for about 1.5 miles to a parking lot. Walk east, cross the road and onto the prairie ahead, aiming toward a large dead tree. This tree denotes the descent into a gully with numerous formations. Explore on your own or consult *Vedauwoo Bouldering* by Davin Bagdonas.

## Cheyenne Frontier Days

World's Largest Rodeo & Western Celebration    www.cfdrodeo.com

Cheyenne Frontier Days started in 1897 and continues every year during the last full week of July. The $1 million in prize money is the biggest purse after the National Finals Rodeo in Las Vegas. Every performance boasts bull rides, bareback rides, saddle bronc rides, rookie saddle bronc rides and a wild horse race. Tour a Native American village and view western art at the Old West Museum, watch grand parades and partake of a free pancake breakfast. The Carnival Midway at Frontier Park offers kids' rides, games, music and food. The USAF Thunderbirds perform aerial acrobatics during Frontier Days.

## Jubilee Days

Laramie has its big rodeo/ranch week, called Jubilee Days, during early July. They hold professional competitions during that time and also host a carnival and parade, not to mention XTREME Bull Riding.
www.laramiejubileedays.com

## Sierra Trading Post (...we know this is shopping, but you just have to go)

5025 Campstool Rd, Cheyenne

(307) 775-8090         www.SierraTradingPost.com

If after leaving home you discover that you've forgotten to bring water bottles or a headlamp, try the Sierra Trading Post. This outlet store carries primarily hiking clothing and supplies, but also has some running and climbing items including GPS wrist computers, brand name tents and backpacks, hydration systems, sleeping bags, camping cookware sets, and more.

## Cheyenne Depot Museum

Number One Depot Square, 121 West 15th Street, Cheyenne

Call for hours      (307) 632-3905      www.cheyennedepotmuseum.org

The museum provides a study of the evolution of locomotives from steam engines to today's diesels, as well as how the railroad system expanded.

REST DAY
ACTIVITIES

### Big Country Speedway

4820 S. Greeley Hwy. (Highway 85), Cheyenne
(307) 632-2107   www.bigcountryspeedway.com
The summer season, beginning the first week of May, is packed with special events. Call ahead to see what categories the nightly races include, perhaps anything from Junk Yard Warriors to Dwarf Cars. When in Rome...

**Sibylle's Travels**
**Terry Bison Ranch**

I recently met two Swiss families traveling with their four kids; the older ones climbed 5.12s. On their way to Devil's Tower, they planned to spend several days riding and playing at a Wyoming dude ranch.

### Terry Bison Ranch

51 I-25 Service Road East, Cheyenne, WY  82007
(307) 634-4171   www.terrybisonranch.com
The Terry Bison Ranch, located about seven miles south of Cheyenne, comprises 30,000 acres of rolling grasslands and houses about 2,500 American Bison (buffalo) including calves every spring. The motorized bison tour travels into the middle of a herd. Also on the scene are horses, longhorn steer, camels, llamas, ostriches, emu, chickens, turkeys, turkins (1/2 turkey-1/2 chicken), peacocks, donkeys, goats, beefalo (1/2 buffalo-1/2 steer) and other wild critters. Pony rides can be a big hit with the little kids. Grandma may not want to ride, but the ranch also offers banquets and great food at Senator's Steakhouse.

### University of Wyoming Art Museum

UW Art Museum, 2111 Willett Drive, Laramie, WY  82071
(307) 766-6622   www.uwyo.edu/ArtMuseum
Free admission. This premier destination for art of the American West was established in 1972 to collect and exhibit visual arts and cultural artifacts. Internationally acclaimed architect Antoine Predock designed the Centennial Complex at the University of Wyoming where the museum is located.

OTHER
CLIMBING
GUIDES

*Rock Climbing at Vedauwoo, Wyoming: Climbs of the Eastern Medicine Bow National Forest*, Robert B. Kelman, 2004.
*Fat Crack Country: Rock Climbing in Vedauwoo*, Zack Orenczak, 2004.
*Vedauwoo Bouldering*, Davin Bagdonas, 2005.

EMERGENCY
INFO
&
MORE

**H**

| Cheyenne | Laramie |
|---|---|
| **Cheyenne Surgical Center** | **Ivinson Memorial Hospital** |
| 3235 Sparks Rd, Cheyenne | 255 N 30th St, Laramie |
| (307) 633-8121 | (307) 742-2141 |

For rescue facilities, call Laramie Ranger District, (307) 745-2300

# WALT'S WALL

The following three climbs share the same first pitch, and the same rappel descent. On the second pitch, ascending straight up provides the hardest finish; the right a bit easier; and the left easier yet.

**Approach**: From the picnic area, walk past the gazebo toward the cliff. To reach the climbs at Walt's Wall, veer left and head uphill, picking your way through the boulders to the base of Walt's Wall.

 **Warning:** There is some scrambling to reach the base. Rappeling skills needed to descend.

### ___1. Edward's Crack, Left Exit 5.4 ★

This route ascends the obvious crack that goes straight up, crosses some ledges and surmounts a bulge near the top.

**P1**. Surmount about 15 feet of tricky moves up A leaning, left-facing dihedral to a much easier crack above. Follow the main crack, cross the first ledge and make some face moves to enter the crack above. Cross another crack and belay (gear) on a ledge at the third crack, about 20 feet below the offwidth slot.

**P2**. For the left exit, follow the crack/ledge left and the head up the face past a bolt to the top.

Tristan Hechtel on *Edward's Crack* 5.4

Walt's Wall

### ___2. Edward's Crack, Center 5.7- ★

This is the direct line.

**P1**. As for Route #1.

**P2**. From the belay ledge, continue straight up to the offwidth slot. Ascend this using armlocks, fist jams (if your hands are big enough), and heel-toe or knee-foot jams, depending on your size. This may be easier for little skinny kids since they can chimney up inside the slot. However, if they've never done a chimney, you may want to opt for another finish. A #4 Camalot would make the leader happy.

### ___3. Edward's Crack, Right Exit 5.5 ★

**P1**. As for Route #1.

**P2**. From the belay, traverse right to the crack just right of the roof. Follow this crack to the top. This finish ends closest to the rappel anchors and eliminates some traversing to reach the descent.

**Descent:** Walk right (climber's right; northeast) along the top of the cliff until you see rappel rings and an extra large bolt you can clip into. Descend with one rope (three rappels) from here. The first rappel ends on a comfortable ledge below the top rappel anchor. The second rappel traverses slightly left (climber's left; away from the big offwidth corner) to an anchor on another good ledge. From here, rappel to the ground.

Edward's Crack

# FALL WALL

Fall Wall is a nice friction slab right of Walt's Wall and separated from it by a protruding buttress called the Coke Bottle. It contains two great short moderates that are safe to lead. The base is guarded by an enormous ribbed boulder appropriately named the Clam Shell. To reach Fall Wall climb over or under this boulder.

**Approach:** From the picnic area, walk past the gazebo toward the Clam Shell. Getting to the base of the Clam Shell is very easy. The scramble past the Clam Shell is slippery, awkward and not easy for very small children. Tunnel under the Clam Shell to its right end and scramble up to the ledge at the base of the Fall Wall climbs. The base of Fall Wall is unsafe for very young kids. The easiest way to reach the climbs on the Fall Wall may be for the most experienced person to scramble to the top of the Clam Shell, then set up a toprope for the route on the face of the Clam Shell (bring a couple of long slings).

Fall Wall

### ___4. Clam Shell 5.5 X

This route is entirely unprotected, so is best toproped. The safest way to set up a toprope is to scramble to the base of Fall Wall and lower a rope from there.

The start provides its greatest challenge. A boost may get the littlest ones off the ground, after which they can friction right up the ribs of this rock. Once everyone topropes this climb, they're in a good position for more routes above.

### ___5. Easy Overhang Lieback 5.5 ★

This is the right-facing, right-leaning corner that starts near the left side of the top of the Clam Shell. Simply layback the crack.

**Descent.** Rappel from here with one rope. You can also toprope the climb from this anchor.
**Pro**: Small TCUs and nuts protect the crack, which ends at a two-bolt anchor.

Climber on *Clam Shell* 5.5

### ___6. Cold Finger 5.7 ★

At the right end of the top of the Clam Shell, there is a fun bolted face climb. Don't mistake this for the bolted route on the arête even further right, which is harder (5.9+, marked "no" in the picture on preceding page).

Climb up the face on small edges and friction, past four bolts to a bolted anchor. Toprope this climb with one rope from this anchor.

### ___7. Easy Overhang Friction 5.5 R ★

Just right of *Easy Overhang Lieback* a pair of bolts shadows a weakness up the slab. This is pretty runout as a lead. If you do lead it, when you get to the top, go either to the *Easy Overhang Lieback* anchors and belay from there, or alternatively traverse right to the next anchors at the top of *Cold Finger*. If you've already led *Easy Overhang Lieback*, it is simple to toprope this climb from the anchors.

Tristan Hechtel on *Cold Finger* 5.7
The crack behind the climber is *Easy Overhang Lieback*

## NAUTILUS

**Approach:** After turning onto Vedauwoo Road, don't turn left into the campground but instead continue straight on a dirt road for 0.2 miles to free parking below the Nautilus, at the trailhead to the Nautilus. Head toward the southwest end of the Nautilus and skirt the base of the rock, heading up through boulders to reach the base of the climb (some scrambling to reach the base). The climb starts at a larger chimney behind a big pine tree or a smaller finger crack that curves up and right from the same start as the chimney.

### ___8. Cornelius 5.5 ★★★

Short but very sweet. *Cornelius* is one of the most enjoyable easy cracks I've done here: no strenuous jams, no offwidths, just thin crack climbing at its finest. If teaching friends or kids how to climb a finger crack is your goal, you can't find a better crack to start them on.

**P1**. Climb up perfect rock, smearing your feet on face holds while holding on with excellent finger locks.

**Pro**: Protect this crack with wired stoppers and small TCUs.

**Descent**: No fixed anchor. Lower the kids and friends, and one person will have to walk off the back side. To walk off, traverse left and thread your way down among the boulders.

### ___9. Easy Jam 5.4

Once you're all the way up here, you might as well climb the big crack left of *Cornelius*. It's a bit of a grunt, but a good value.

**Descent**: Same as *Cornelius*.

Jaclyn Paik, age 7, on **Gina's Surprise** 5.4

# ESTES PARK AREA AND ROCKY MOUNTAIN NATIONAL PARK

More people visit Rocky Mountain National Park than any other Colorado park for a reason—incredibly beautiful scenery and gorgeous views. Snow-capped peaks surround clear alpine lakes, alpine flowers paint the meadows bright purple and yellow in summer, and golden aspen trees decorate the hills in fall. Accessible hikes allow easy access to gorgeous waterfalls and creeks where marmots and elk play.

There are two areas here with excellent moderate climbing, both close to the town of Estes Park—Lumpy Ridge, just a mile north of town, and Jurassic Park, a few miles south of Estes Park on Highway 7 (The Peak to Peak road), near the turn-off to Longs Peak.

Head to Lumpy Ridge for three- to five-pitch easy routes on sublime granite. Lumpy Ridge granite is clean, protects well with an abundance of cracks, isn't too rough and gritty, nor is it too polished and slippery. Numerous routes in the 5.4 to 5.7 range provide days of pleasant crack and slab climbing with generally spacious belay ledges.

The approach hikes can be long, but worth it. I've climbed on the Pear with a family with three girls. The two-year old enjoyed the dirt at the base and the older kids (around age nine) enjoyed the climbing. My father hiked in to climb at Lumpy when he was in his seventies.

The Pear is the lowest of the cliffs, with the flattest approach, and sports several high-quality climbs. The Book looks closer, but sits higher up and thus entails a steeper approach hike. There is a collection of high-quality climbs on the Left Book and some topropable shorter routes on The Book.

The very beauty and desirability of this area also creates its greatest drawback: crowds. Climbing at Lumpy Ridge on a weekend can mean both full parking lots and routes. Lines abound at campgrounds, stores, and in traffic. If possible, plan a trip during the week and both parking and getting on the routes tend to be much easier.

Jurassic Park, on the road towards The Crags, offers great face and sport climbing with numerous well-bolted routes of 100 feet or less. The local climbing schools often bring their classes here, so you may have company. From Jurassic Park, enjoy the great views of Lily Lake and the distant Diamond on Longs Peak.

For those climbers uncertain about finding the climbs, or who would prefer to follow the longer multi-pitch routes, the Colorado Mountain School ((970) 586-5758) will guide you and your party at many of the cliffs here.

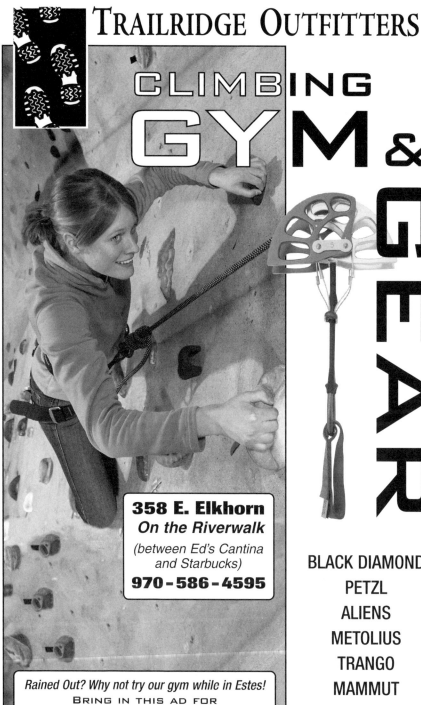

# TRAILRIDGE OUTFITTERS

## CLIMBING GYM & GEAR

**358 E. Elkhorn**
*On the Riverwalk*
(between Ed's Cantina
and Starbucks)
**970-586-4595**

BLACK DIAMOND
PETZL
ALIENS
METOLIUS
TRANGO
MAMMUT
& much more

*Rained Out? Why not try our gym while in Estes!*
BRING IN THIS AD FOR
**$4.⁰⁰ OFF CLIMBING GYM**

## The Thumbs Up and Thumbs Down on Estes Park/RMNP Area.....

 **Pros:** Gorgeous views and beautiful scenery; high quality routes on good rock; peaceful and quiet mid-week; interesting wildlife (elk, marmots, and ptarmigan); Rocky Mountain National Park; Estes Park has all amenities and many fun activities for kids.

 **Cons:** Long approaches; afternoon thunderstorms; crowded climbs and parking on weekends; traffic.

## Climbing here is mostly...

## Logistics at a Glance

Approach

30 minutes to an hour depending on the chosen cliff.

Food?

Estes Park has many options. See text for more details.

Rock Type

Granite
with great friction

Cell Coverage

Yes, at Lumpy Ridge

Climb Type

Mostly gear at Lumpy
Some sport at Jurassic Park

Hot Spots

Estes Deli, 361 S. St. Vrain;
Kind Coffee, free w/purchase,
470 E. Elkhorn Ave;
Notch Top Cafe, 457 E. Wonderview

Ages

Best for ages 8-9 and up due to the hike, environment and multi-pitch requirements.

Dogs?

No, not allowed in National Parks

Camping?

RMNP, four busy campgrounds at the east side of the park. Some take reservations. Commercial sites available around Estes Park. See camping section for more details.

Seasons

Summer
(Spring and Fall can be good)

## How many routes are here?*

| | | |
|---|---|---|
| 5.0-5.6 | | 30+ |
| 5.7 | | 30+ |
| 5.8 | | 30+ |
| 5.9 | | 30+ |

* This statistic is for reference only, not all climbs of these grades have been chosen for this book.

GETTING
THERE

**From Denver or Boulder**, take US 36 to Lyons and continue on US 36 another 19 miles past Lyons to Estes Park.

**From Fort Collins**, drive up W. Eisenhower Blvd/US-34 for 27 miles.

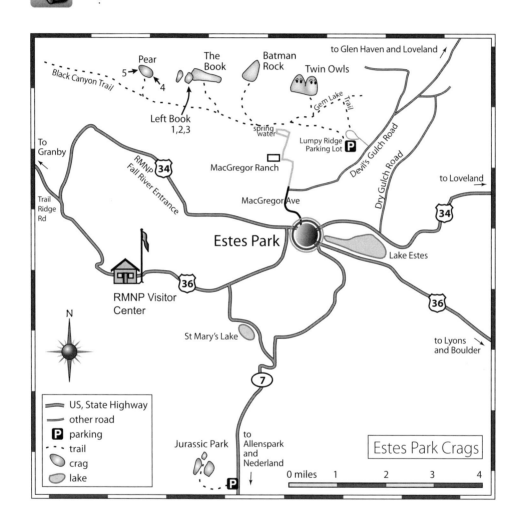

**Warning:** The number of easy routes here may be misleading since most of the climbs are multi-pitch with a long approach hike and sometimes with a devious descent. While the actual climbing may not be technically difficult, the climbs are in a semi-alpine environment with potential afternoon thunderstorms, route finding difficulties, and a long hike out. With this in mind a 5.6 in this area feels potentially more serious than a 5.8 sport climb with a short approach and descent by lowering off.

SETTING UP
CAMP

**Sibylle's Travels
Great Reference**

A good camping
reference is *The Best
in Tent Camping Colo-
rado: A Guide for Car
Campers who Hate RVs,
Concrete Slabs, and Loud
Portable Stereos*, Johnny
Molloy, 2001. Mol-
loy includes Longs
Peak campground
among his selection
of 50 best tent
camping places in
the state.

## Rocky Mountain National Park

The Park Service runs four campgrounds at the east side of the park,
described below. All tend to fill up on busy summer weekends, so arrive
early or reserve well ahead of time. There are no electric, water or sewer
hookups at any camp sites. www.nps.gov

1. **Longs Peak**. Near the trailhead to Longs Peak, the 26 sites are first
come/first served. Set among pines in a scenic setting, this campground
permits only tents. Summer camping costs $20. In fall through spring,
when no water is available, the fee is $14. There is a seven night limit in
summer; fourteen nights in winter. Information: (970) 586-1206.

2. **Glacier Basin**. This is 7.0 miles west of the Beaver Meadows Visitor
Center off of Bear Lake Road. Most sites are in a lodgepole pine forest.
The camping fee is $20 per night per site. Reservations recommended.
1-877-444-6777 or www.recreation.gov.

3. **Moraine Park**. Moraine Park Campground is located off of the Bear
Lake Road, near the Beaver Meadows Visitor Center. Sites are mainly in
a ponderosa pine forest and look out over Moraine Park. During the summer, the fee is $20. From fall through spring, when no water is available,
the fee drops to $14. Reservations are accepted at 1-877-444-6777 or
www.recreation.gov.

4. **Aspenglen**. This campground has 54 first come/first served sites along
Fall River, 5.0 miles west of Estes Park. Fee is $20 per night. Information:
(970) 586-1206

## Mary's Lake Campground

You can also find a number of commercial campgrounds surrounding Estes
Park. If you visit in an RV, you might enjoy staying at Mary's Lake Campground, near Mary's Lake, just above town and close to climbing at Lily Lake.

Tristan Hechtel on *Coloradoddity* 5.5

HOTELS & MOTELS

**Stanley Hotel**, 333 W Wonderview Ave, Estes Park.
(970) 586-3371     www.stanleyhotel.com
If you want to indulge your family, you can't beat the historic Stanley Hotel, which hosted the emperor of Japan a few years ago.

**Holiday Inn Hotel**, 101 S. St. Vrain, Estes Park.
(970) 586-2332     www.HolidayInn.com
If you just want a shower and a night to get clean after camping, the Holiday Inn has a nice indoor pool and convenient location. Most chains up here provide free high speed Internet.

Numerous motels and most chains have a branch here, thus if camping turns to *hoteling it*, lodging shouldn't be a major concern.

SHOPPING & GROCERIES

Depending on your attitude toward shopping, Estes Park is either a shopper's mecca or a tourist trap. In this gateway to the Rockies, quaint shoppes selling homemade fudge, salt-water taffy, Native American crafts, and T-shirts line both sides of the main drag. For more prosaic needs, try the stores below.

**Safeway**, 451 E. Wonderview Ave, (970) 586-4447

**Trailridge Outfitters**, 358 E. Elkhorn, (970) 586-4595

**Komito Boots**, 235 W. Riverside Dr. (downtown area), (970) 586-5391
Should your climbing shoes fall apart while on this trip, Steve Komito has been resoling rock shoes for decades. Steve will willingly give you route descriptions and general background information on the area.

RESTAURANTS & COFFEE

**Notch Top Café**, 457 E. Wonderview, (970) 586-0272
Many climbers breakfast at the Notch Top, named after a local mountain. They sell delicious pastries with which I've bribed my son to carry the rope.

**Ed's Cantina**, 366 E. Elkhorn Ave, (970) 586-2919
Another local climber's hangout, where you may find information on routes, conditions, and local events. I've eaten decent, but not spectacular, Mexican food here. Local climbers like the snacks at the bar.

**Macdonald Papeterie**, 150 East Elkhorn Ave, (970) 586-3451
A good coffee place, run by climbers.

**Estes Deli & Catering Co.**, 1110 Woodstock, (970) 586-5741

**Kind Coffee**, 470 E. Elkhorn Ave, (970) 586-5206

Tyrolean Traverse at Jurássic Park

# What Else Can We Do That's Fun?

BOULDERING

### Bouldering

The boulderfields which surround Estes Park can inspire exploration. Bouldering near Lumpy Ridge is a fine way to end the day or a great way to begin the day if the weather looks dubious. Many fine boulders are strewn amid the trees about 0.7 miles northwest from the new Lumpy Ridge parking lot. If you'd like the V-ratings and problem names, consult *Colorado Bouldering* and *Colorado Bouldering 2* by Benningfield/Samet.

REST DAY
ACTIVITIES

### Climbing Gyms

If it rains while you're in Estes Park, retreat to a rock gym. It may help with acclimatization—and what a great place to teach the kids.

#### Trailridge Outfitters

358 E. Elkhorn Avenue     www.trailridgeoutfitters.com     (970) 586-4595
Trailridge Outfitters is easy to find (on the main drag between Ed's Cantina and Starbucks) and has a climbing wall in the back of their outdoor gear shop. They stock a full selection of climbing and camping gear, as well as renting climbing shoes, harnesses and camping equipment. A climbing day pass or a bouldering day pass could rescue your afternoon if the thunderstorms roll in.

#### Estes Park Mountain Shop

2050 Big Thompson Canyon, (970) 586-6548
This shop has a bit larger climbing wall. It's just outside of Estes Park, a little way down the canyon towards Loveland.

**Onward**

### Hiking

Maureen Keilty, in her book *Best Hikes With Children in Colorado,* describes three great hikes in Rocky Mountain National Park as being among the 75 best hikes with kids in Colorado. All require payment of a fee to enter the park ($20 per car for a 7-day entry or buy an annual National Parks Pass $80).

**Sibylle's Travels**
**Great Reference**
*Best Hikes With Children in Colorado* by Maureen Keilty is a great travel gem. You may consider packing it along with your climbing gear. If the kids tire of climbing, but some of the adults want another pitch or two, this book can provide a nearby hike.

The Bear Lake loop offers you the choice between a 0.5 mile or a 5.6 mile loop, a nice alternative for very small (or tired) kids, or older relatives. Enter the Park on US 36 and drive on the Bear Lake Road to the Bear Lake parking lot, where the trail starts at the west end of the lot. A paved, level half-mile interpretive loop around Bear Lake describes the high mountain lake ecology in a self-guiding trail booklet. Another alternative is to add a little more at a time, starting with the half-mile walk to Nymph Lake.

Keilty also describes hikes to Sprague Lake, only 0.5 mile south of the Bear Lake shuttle bus parking. This trail is wheelchair accessible and the park provides wheelchair accessible toilet and water at the Sprague Lake parking lot.

REST DAY
ACTIVITIES

### Horseback Riding

Several stables can either take the younger kiddos on pony rides or the older ones on overnight pack trips.

**Cowpoke Corner Corral & National Park Gateway Stables**
(970) 586-5890 and (970) 586-5269    www.cowpokecornercorral.com

**Aspen Lodge** 6120 Highway 7, 1-800-332-6867, (970) 586-8133
Located about eight miles south of Estes Park. Aspen Lodge offers hay rides, sleigh rides, and an overnight pack trip.

### Other Attractions

**Cascade Arcade and Cascade Creek Mini-Golf**
Mall Road and Hwy. 34 (by Estes Park City limit sign)    (970) 586-6495
We play mini-golf here all the time. If you get the golf ball into the correct hole at the end, you win another round of the game. In addition to mini-golf, they also offer a train ride for little kids, bumper cars, bumper boats, and go-karts.

**Fun City**, 455 Prospect Village Dr.
(970) 586-2828 and (970) 586-2070    www.funcityofestes.com
This is near Elkhorn Avenue & Moraine (Hwy 36). On a hot day, cool off sliding down the 42-foot high water slide and dry off playing arcade games afterwards.

**MacGregor Ranch Museum**    (970) 586-3749
When done climbing at Lumpy, why not visit the museum on your way out? Tour an 1896 manor house, with clothes, utensils, china, and pictures in every room much like they were back then.

---

### Sibylle's Travels
**Baby Travel Tip**

**Baby Rental Equipment**

*Traveling Babies*
(970) 577.1277
travelingbabies.com

For folks who fly in and rent a car, Traveling Babies will provide backpacks and many other outdoor accessories.

---

OTHER
CLIMBING
GUIDES

*Rocky Mountain National Park: The Climber's Guide; Estes Park Valley*, Gillett, 2001.
*The Park: A Guide to the High Peaks and Crags of RMNP*, Fred Knapp and Mike Stevens, 1998.
*Rock Climbing Colorado*, Stewart Green, 1995.
*Rock Climbing: Rocky Mountain National Park; The Crag Areas*, Richard Rossiter, 1996.
*Front Range Topropes*, Fred Knapp, 2000.

EMERGENCY
INFO
&
MORE

### Estes Park
**Estes Park Medical Center**          **Estes Park Public Library**
555 Prospect Ave.                      335 E Elkhorn Ave.
(970) 586-2317                         (970) 586-8116  www.estes.lib.co.us

# LUMPY RIDGE

Lumpy Ridge has a fabulous selection of sunny climbs, on perfect granite, in a beautiful setting. Protection is mostly nuts and cams. An early start is advised, both to avoid crowds and avoid the regular—and sometimes sudden—summer afternoon thunderstorms. Bring a waterproof parka and an extra sweater, just in case.

**Approach:** From the Hwy 34/36 intersection in downtown Estes Park, continue on Hwy 34 past the Stanley Hotel. Turn north on MacGregor Ave. which becomes Devils Gulch Rd. Head 0.75 miles north following the road as it will bend 90 degrees to the right (east). Continue another 0.5 miles east, and follow signs directing you left onto the Lumpy Ridge parking lot access road. Trail access is found on either side of the toilet facilities. On the left side is a trailhead heading west to all the climbing areas. The trail passes through a low saddle in the forest and continue another 0.25 miles where you'll find a memorial drinking fountain with crisp spring water in the summer.

After hiking about 25 minutes look for a sign marking a fork in the trail. The sign "Climber Access to the Book Area" designates the righthand fork and the left turn continues as "Black Canyon Trail". Turn right and head uphill, following signs to the Book. At the next fork, a sign directs you to turn left toward the "Bookmark". At your third and final sign, turn right towards the Bookmark and Left Book. The left fork here leads to the Bookend. Follow a rocky climber's trail uphill along the left side of the Bookmark to the large obvious slabs that comprise the Left Book.

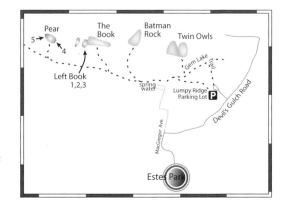

# Left Book

The Left Book has some great climbs following flakes and cracks up a superb slab.
Base of cliff, GPS: 13 T 0454485 UTH 4472969 (before gully)

 **Hazards:** Thundershowers, possible rockfall.

Three climbs go up the middle of the slab, *White Whale*, *Hiatus*, and *Manifest Destiny*. You can climb almost anywhere you like on this face and combine different pitches from different climbs among these three routes. I'll describe what I consider the two best routes.

____**1. White Whale** 5.7 ★★
Head for the slabs comprising the Left Book. You'll see a prominent, long, narrow roof with a pine tree above the left end of the roof.

**P1.** Climb up a crack and flake to the left edge of the roof. Belay at the ledge with a pine tree (you can climb the first pitch of *Hiatus* instead).

**P2.** Step left, climb a left-facing corner to a straight-in crack. Climb the crack until it ends and then traverse left to a path left of a shallow corner.

**P3.** Follow corners and cracks up and left to Paperback Ledge, a large ledge with big trees.

**Descent:** Walk left (north) on Paperback Ledge until you see a faint climber's trail heading down. Follow this, easy scrambling, to the base of the Left Book.

Left Book

45

### ____2. Hiatus 5.7 ★★★

This excellent route is a perhaps a tad harder than *White Whale*. Start just right of *White Whale*.

**P1.** Climb up left-facing flakes and corners to a crack that ends about 10 feet right of the left edge of the roof. Traverse left below the roof and layback up the left-facing corner to a ledge with a pine tree.

**P2.** Traverse right about 20–25 feet to a left-facing corner with a big crack. Layback up this corner. You'll need a large cam for the bottom of this corner, or you can run it out and get smaller cams (#2 and smaller) in the top half of the crack. Continue up this corner until it ends and then traverse left below a small roof; then head up and left to belay in a small alcove.

**P3.** Follow a corner up and heading left to Paperback Ledge.

**Descent:** See descent for *White Whale*.

**Additional Gear Suggestion:** Bring a #3 or #4 Camalot for pitch 2.

Tristan Hechtel bouldering on Jaws Boulder, Lumpy Ridge

### ____3. Manifest Destiny 5.7 ★

If people are on the two routes described above, *Manifest Destiny* provides a worthwhile, if less classic, alternative. Start left of *Hiatus*, at the base of a flake system.

**P1.** Climb flakes left of *Hiatus* to a ledge about 30 ft. left of the pine tree belay of *Hiatus*. Belay on ledge about 30 feet left of the *White Whale* belay ledge.

**P2.** Climb up a right-facing corner and then move left on a crack at the top and then back right to a ledge (if you continue traversing left here, you can climb up a more difficult (5.8) right-facing corner). Belay here.

**P3.** From the ledge, climb up easy face and flakes, left of *Hiatus*, to Paperback Ledge.

**Descent:** See descent for *White Whale*.

Tristan Hechtel comments on sleeping at the base: "Learning to bivy on ledges, legs inside one climbing pack with a second pack as a pillow, provides good training for future big wall climbing."

Noemi on White Whale 5.7    Photograph by Tristan Hechtel

## The Pear

The Pear is a friendly slabby buttress, a little beyond The Book area. As with Left Book, watch for afternoon thunderstorms, and bring some extra clothing. The base area is safe and flat and I've seen two-year-olds playing at the base.

**Approach:** From the Lumpy Ridge Parking Lot head west past the old lot and the water fountain. Continue along the lower trail towards The Book. You will pass a sign *Black Canyon Trail Lawn Lake*. After about 15 minutes, go through a gate. On the far side, a sign marks a fork in the trail. *Climber Access to the Book Area* designates the right-hand fork while the left path continues as *Black Canyon Trail*. Stay left here on a relatively flat trail for another 5–8 minutes. After about 30 minutes total, you will arrive at a sign, *The Pear*. Turn right here and start hiking gently uphill. After about 35 minutes you'll be directly below The Pear. Before you arrive at the cliff, the trail branches, with an indistinct fork heading right toward *Gina's Surprise* and the other, left fork, heading to several 5.6 to 5.7 slab climbs including *La Chaim* and *Magical Chrome Plated Semi-Automatic Enema Syringe* (it's a good climb, despite the odd name). After you head right, continue fairly level for a bit and then start hiking more steeply uphill on an indistinct climber's trail. Pass a large corner and head up toward an amazing huge dike on the shoulder, about another 2–3 minutes.

____**4. Gina's Surprise** 5.4 R ★★

This five-pitch climb starts at the base of the dike on the right end of The Pear. Many people climb just the first pitch. You can also traverse off rightwards from one of the upper ledge belays or you can continue for several pitches to the summit. The upper easy pitches go quickly and are lots of fun with splendid views as you ascend.

**P1.** Climb up the huge dike for about 100 ft. to a large tree. The climbing to the tree is only 5.4, but fairly runout near the bottom. You can place an RP and some small cams down low. Set up a toprope at the tree, using long slings and a 60-meter rope. To descend from here, you can lower the toproping climbers but the last person has to climb up and right to another tree and a ledge, then walk off right to the descent gully.

Pear Buttress viewed from the east

Kira Paik, 9, on *Gina's Surprise* 5.4

**P2.** Continue climbing up the dike to a tree (190 ft, bring a #3.5 and/or #4 Friend for the belay). To escape from here, you can traverse off right on a wide ledge that joins an easy descent gully.

**P3.** Follow the dike, climb an awkward right-arching crack system and then traverse slightly right on a broad ledge. Belay at a huge tree (190 ft). To escape from this ledge, a short (40 ft) rappel from a tree reaches the descent gully.

**P4.** Romp up another long pitch to a nook/recess (190 ft).

**P5.** Continue all the way to a bolted belay/rappel anchor at the top (100 ft.). You can rappel or lower to the ground 80 ft. or so.

**Descent:** Refer to individual pitch descriptions.

The line of *Gina's Surprise*

### ____5. Magical Chrome Plated Semi-Automatic Enema Syringe 5.7 ★★★

At the base of the wall, far left of *Gina's Surprise*, look for a large block below a left-facing dihedral. This is a fine route for children that know how to climb 5.7 very comfortably, and even better if they can climb harder routes and are used to exposure.

**P1.** Scramble up this block and then climb one of the cracks above the block. Climb any one of several cracks on Pitch 1. Each traverses left, with the lowest being the hardest. Traverse left along a flake (protect this for the second) to the belay. Or, traverse left higher up along an obvious ramp.

**P2.** Climb the right-facing corner to a ledge. Follow this ledge left to a belay. It's possible to continue up several more pitches, but most people traverse left on this ledge to where there's a walk off to the left.

**Descent:** After scrambling leftwards on the ledge, you will reach the easy gully left (west) of the crag. Hike down here to the base.

I took my son up this when he was seven, in a party of three: one led the group, then my son followed, and lastly a third to take out the gear. When taking a beginner, consider that they need to remove the cams and nuts and may find it difficult or frightening to do so if they aren't used to doing this. I found this one of the more challenging issues when taking my small son up climbs. He could climb the rock fine, but he initially struggled with removing gear.

Kira and Jaclyn Paik on the belay ledge at the top of the 1st pitch of *Gina's Surprise*.

**Suggestion:** I wouldn't take a kid who's only climbed indoors on this route. Without a third person, you risk losing some gear. Running it out isn't really an option on this climb, due to the protection necessary for the second on the traversing sections.

# LILY LAKE - JURASSIC PARK

This area is beautifully situated in a quiet pine forest above a pretty lake. Mostly well-bolted moderate sport climbs can be found here, with many opportunities for toproping. Check out www.mountainproject.com for several new routes by prominent developer Rick Thompson.

**Approach:** Drive south from Estes Park on Hwy. 7 and park at the Lily Lake Visitor Center or across the road (about 6.0 miles, just past mile marker 6). Walk up the hiker's trail that starts at the southeast end of Lily Lake, beside the footbridge, for about 15 minutes. Continue uphill on the trail until it flattens and tends slightly downhill. At a large cairn, turn right and head up a steep, scree-filled climber's trail for another 10–15 minutes until you can see the cliffs.

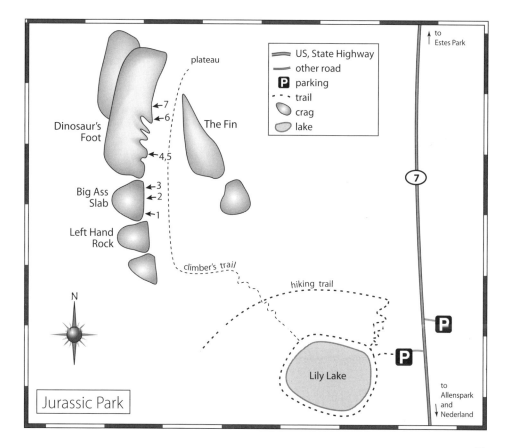

# Big Ass Slab

The first rock on your left, aptly named Left Hand Rock, features two gear climbs (not described). The next dome on the left is called Big Ass Slab. It features several excellent bolted climbs on high quality rock. The base of the climbs lies directly next to the trail where you can make basecamp on some flat spots.

### ____6. Coloradoddity 5.5 ★★★

Rick Thompson hails this one of the best routes of its grade in Colorado, combining great rock and solid bolts, topped with a view of the Diamond. This is the first bolted route seen as you hike up the main access gully. Begin at the left edge of the main face.

Big Ass Slab

Follow the line of clips up the rounded, low-angled prow and slab above to anchors. An encouraging fact for novice climbers is that the crux is passing the second bolt; after this the angle decreases and the climbing gets much easier. The anchors have rappel rings.

**Pro:** Nine clips, 85 feet.

### Variation Start 5.6 ★★ TR

Climb the rib 10 feet left of the normal start and join the route at mid-height.

### ____7. The Stout Blue Vein 5.7+ ★★

The second bolted route you come to. Begin 10 feet right of *Coloradoddity* and climb the face. At the second bolt, traverse right along a rising crack, clip the third bolt, and then head straight up to anchors.

**Pro:** Seven clips. 85 feet.

### Variation Finish 5.6 ★★

At the second bolt head straight up to join Coloradoddity.

### ____8. Assmosis 5.8+ ★★

 Start under a flake, just right of a line of bolts (*Critical Morass* 5.10c).

Climb the left-facing flake until it ends. Clip a bolt, and ascend the ramp (possible pro). Clip the second bolt, and climb the slab past three more bolts to anchors shared with *Critical Morass* (95 feet, 60-meter rope needed).

**Pro:** Cams up to #3 protect the initial flake, with four bolts on the face.

# Dinosaur's Foot

The next crag up from Big Ass Slab, the Dinosaur's Foot, features several routes and is where the local guides take their classes for toproping.

____**9. Index Toe**  5.8 ★★
On the southeast face of the crag there's a line of bolts up the leftmost rib. Follow bolts up the face, with a crux move between bolts 5 and 6. The route is well-bolted lower down where it's more difficult and runout near the top when the climbing gets easier.
**Pro:** Eight clips, 2-bolt anchor.

____**10. Middle Toe**  5.9- ★★★
This route is located on the second bolted arête from the left on Dinosaur's Foot. The climbing is similar to *Index Toe* but more sustained, with technical moves near the bottom and three or four bolts before the anchors. This route can be toproped after leading *Index Toe* to enjoy continuous moves on quality rock.
**Pro:** Nine bolts, 2-bolt anchor (shared with *Index Toe*).

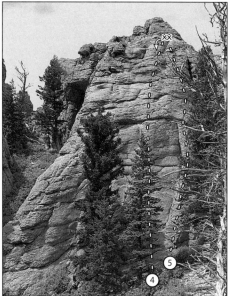

Dinosaur's Foot

Tristan Hechtel on *Coloradoddity* 5.5

## Toprope Wall Area

Continue uphill toward the saddle. On your left, just before a curving crack in the face, there are two more bolted climbs. You may also see a few guides with clients here. When I've encountered them, they've been pleasant and helpful, and offered to let us use their topropes or move any ropes in our way.

Toprope Wall

____**11. Strategery** 5.7- ★

Access a prominent slot or groove by traversing in left from the right. Climb the crack and slabby wall past bolts to the two-bolt anchor. Some lichen on the rock makes smearing more exciting. **Pro:** Four clips, 35 feet.

____**12. Toprope Wall Crack** 5.7/5.8 ★

Lead the obvious arching crack using gear. Or you can toprope it. To set up a toprope, lead the easier *Stategery*, then scramble up and right to the anchors.

Traverse in to the crack from the right and then follow it until it ends. At this point, you can continue traversing left, or head right and up (see photo) for a more direct finish.

Dagny on *Toprope Wall Crack* 5.7/5.8

Brian Doub on Castle Rock West Face 5.5

# BOULDER CANYON AND ELDORADO CANYON

When I was climbing in Yosemite in the 80s, a friend told me the country's three world-class climbing areas were Yosemite, Eldorado Canyon, and the Shawangunks. Yosemite remains one of the world's top destination climbing areas where climbers speak languages or with accents from six continents. Back in the late 70s and early 80s, I saw many of Europe's then top climbers visiting Boulder – Patrick Edlinger, Catherine Destivelle and others. Today, with the rise of sport climbing and the incredible rise of housing prices near Boulder, less of the country's top climbers live in Boulder and fewer climbers visit Boulder since camping provides a challenge. For those who don't mind camping farther away, Boulder remains a place well worth visiting.

Within a few minutes of Boulder, climbs abound at Eldorado Canyon, Boulder Canyon, or the Flatirons. I'll discuss Boulder Canyon and Eldorado in detail, since both have easy routes with short approaches, easy descents and a safe flat base area. While the Flatirons form the most dramatic feature in Boulder's skyline, most routes are multi-pitch with relatively long approaches and descents.

Eldorado Canyon with the hamlet of Eldorado Springs in the foreground

GETTING
THERE

**From Denver or Colorado Springs** head on I-25 to the Hwy 36 turnpike. Continue through the Denver burbs heading west for about 20 miles. If Eldorado Canyon is your destination, take the 1st exit off of Hwy 36 onto Table Mesa Drive, turn left toward the mountains, and hook a left on Broadway. Take a right on SH 170 toward the Canyon.

If you're heading up Boulder Canyon, the most straight forward drive is to come into town on Hwy 36 and continue straight as the street becomes the more commercial 28th street. Take a left and head west on Canyon, which eventually heads up Boulder Canyon.

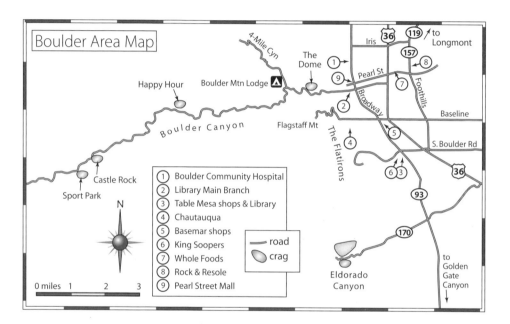

SETTING UP
CAMP

There isn't a great place to camp close to Eldorado Canyon. The nearest location is a small commercial lodge up Boulder Canyon that offers camping. Highly recommended is Golden Gate State Park, about 35 minutes drive away from Boulder.

**Boulder Mountain Lodge**
91 Fourmile Canyon Dr, Boulder.     (303) 444-0882
This lodge provides nine sites with electricity and firepots. They also supply showers and a bathhouse. Rates are $18 per night in summer and go down to $14 per night during the off-season. Boulder County sets a limit of two weeks camping annually. The nearby lodge has 27 rooms with kitchenettes.

57

MORE SETTING
UP CAMP

**Sibylle's Travels
Great Reference**

A good camping reference is *The Best in Tent Camping Colorado: A Guide for Car Campers who Hate RVs, Concrete Slabs, and Loud Portable Stereos*, Johnny Molloy, 2001. Molloy includes a nice description of Golden Gate State Park.

### Golden Gate Canyon State Park

92 Crawford Gulch Road, Golden.     (303) 470-1144

www.parks.state.co.us/Parks/goldengatecanyon

A group of road-tripping climbers told me Golden Gate was the best improved campground for car camping they'd ever stayed in, partly due to the widely spread-out spacious sites. The park lies in the Roosevelt National Forest, at elevations ranging from 7,400 to 10,300 feet and is open year round. Cabins, yurts and guest houses at Reverend's Ridge may be reserved year-round. Campsites here are open in the winter through the self-service station located in the campground. Starting Memorial Day weekend through the end of September reservations must be made with a minimum of three days in advance up to six months in advance.

To get to Golden Gate State Park from Denver, take US 6 towards Golden and then take Highway 93 north from Golden for one mile to Golden Gate Canyon Road. Turn left and continue for 13 miles to the park. From Boulder, drive south on Highway 93 almost to Golden, and watch for the turn off for Golden Gate Canyon Road located one mile north of Golden. Turn right here, and continue 13 miles to the park.

HOTELS &
MOTELS

### Chautauqua, 900 Baseline Road

(303) 442.3282 x -11     www.chautauqua.com

Built in 1898, this is one of three historic Chautauqua communities, retreats that focus on culture, music and nature. The efficiency, one-, two- and three-bedroom cottages have kitchens, but lack TVs and phones. Best of all, you can walk from here to the Flatirons, Gregory Amphitheater, or hike up to Flagstaff for bouldering. Prices range from $87 to $224 a night.

### Boulder Outlook Hotel, 800 28th St.

(303) 443-3322     www.boulderoutlook.com

This family-oriented hotel offers a great place to hang out between out-door activities. The large indoor courtyard in the center of the hotel offers a chlorine-free pool, hot tub, and some free-standing boulders if the kids didn't get enough climbing. This is a pet-friendly hotel complete with a pet park.

### St. Julien Hotel, 900 Walnut St.

(720) 406-9696     www.stjulien.com

This hotel combines a fantastic downtown location, world-class accom-modations and service with dramatic views of the Flatirons. It also has an impressive band lineup, featuring jazz, blues, and dancing to local Salsa band Quemando. Spa treatments are available. This hotel is not exactly priced for the budget vacation.

**King Soopers**,

1650 30th St., (303) 444-0164 **and** 3600 Table Mesa Dr., (303) 499-4004

The Table Mesa King Soopers is across the street from the Reynolds branch of Boulder Public Library. Get your groceries and email all in one trip!

**Wild Oats Natural Marketplace** (Future Whole Foods)

1651 Broadway, (303) 442-0909 **and**

2584 Baseline Rd. at Baseline and Broadway, (303) 499-7636

Quintessential Boulder! This is Boulder's homegrown health food market complete with dinner options, fresh-made sandwiches, and salad bar galore.

**Whole Foods Market**, 2905 Pearl St. (28th and Pearl), (303) 545-6611

A great food shopping experience with lots of prepared goodies to take on your hike or climbing outing.

**Neptune Mountaineering**, 633 South Broadway

(303) 499-8866    www.neptunemountaineering.com

If you need some more carabiners, new climbing shoes, or just want beta on the climbing, Neptune's is your place to go. Plus they have great slide shows, generally on Thursday evening around 8:00 pm but check the schedule just in case. I've heard legendary speakers here like Jim Bridwell, Kurt Diemberger, and Reinhold Messner. Gary Neptune, the owner and an accomplished mountaineer, often presents slideshows and films of his adventures from El Capitan in the 60s to Himalayan ascents.

**Rock and Resole**, 2500 47th St., (303) 440-0414

I've had them resole my climbing shoes since the 80s (and yes, in one case the same pair of shoes that I had for almost 15 years). While they have relatively quick turnover, it's not overnight since the glue (on the soles) needs to dry. They mail shoes after repair, so it's possible to leave climbing shoes with them at the end of the trip.

RESTAURANTS & COFFEE

Restaurants come and go, so rather than focus only on new fashionable places, I'll mention a few places with good food that have been around for years, and sometimes even have reasonable prices. In Boulder, one can get great Indian, Nepali, Thai, Mexican, Japanese, and more.

For more diners who want a more eclectic or extensive overview of the Boulder dining scene, look at Claire Walter's blog, www.culinary-colorado. blogspot.com.

**Himalayas Restaurant**, 2010 14th St., (303) 442-3230
This is one of our favorite Indian/Nepali places, with both excellent vegetarian and Tandoori cuisine. Try a Nan, a filled flat bread, with dinner, like the fruit and nut-filled Khabouli Nan. To cool off, try the mango Lhasi (a yogurt-like drink). It's located just off the Pearl Street Mall, so after finishing dinner walk up the mall for ice cream, cookies, and entertainment.

**Boulder Dushanbe Teahouse**
1770 13th Street, (303) 442-4993      www.boulderteahouse.com
Boulder's sister city, Dushanbe (Tajikistan), donated the exotic glazed tiles and hand-carved wooden ceiling. For those not climbing on Saturday enjoy both brunch as well as the Farmers' Market located right outside.

**Southern Sun**, 627 South Broadway, (303) 543-0886
The brewpub where hippies and climbers go. It's right next to Neptune's, climbing shop extraordinaire. In summer, sit outside at their picnic tables, where sharing with newcomers is encouraged, and enjoy views of the Flatirons while eating. I've enjoyed their raspberry wheat beer, and a friend, who doesn't generally like fruity beers, asked for another sip after he tried it. He, however, prefers the Annapurna amber. They always have a good selection of beers on "nitro", including their Kind amber ale. I've eaten their nachos and Tim's Blackened Chicken Quesadilla, which was very good. They do NOT accept credit cards, so come equipped with cash.

**Walnut Cafe and South Side Walnut Cafe**
3073 Walnut St. (near 29th St. shopping area), (303) 447-2315
**or** 673 S. Broadway (near Neptune Mountaineering), (720) 304-8118
A local favorite sure to serve up a great omelette, waffle, or chicken salad sandwich. Lots of vegetarian options are on the reasonably priced menu.

## Boulder Weekly's Annual Best of Boulder County

### Best Breakfast
**Lucile's:** 2124 14th St., Boulder - (303) 442-4743

**Runner-Up: Walnut Café:**
see above

### Best Burger

**Mountain Sun and Southern Sun:** see above

### Best Place to Bring Kids
**Red Robin:**
2580 Arapahoe Ave.   (303) 442-0320

**Runner-Up: Noodles & CO**
2770 Pearl St., Boulder   (303) 444-5533
1245 Alpine Ave., Boulder   (303) 440-4340
2850 Baseline Rd., Boulder   (303) 247-9978

**Cafe Gondolier**: *Claire's Pick*
1600 Pearl St.   (303) 443-5015

# What Else Can We Do That's Fun?

## Bouldering

With the increase in popularity of bouldering, almost as many climbers come to Boulder for the bouldering as come to climb. Bouldering in Colorado enjoys a long history starting with John Gill and his followers, many of whom bouldered here long ago.

Check out either Flagstaff Mountain or Mount Sanitas for some high-quality bouldering, preferably with a guide in hand. To reach Flagstaff's boulders head west up Baseline Rd. and continue winding up the mountain. Before passing the ranger kiosk on your right pay a small permit fee to park and reset your odometer. Continue 1.2 miles up, hopefully find parking here, and walk south to the most popular cluster of problems.

Alternatively, Mount Sanitas offers a host of mellower problems. From downtown Boulder, head north on Broadway. After several blocks, head west (left) on Mapleton. Pass through the residential area on Mapleton to parking at the trailhead. Hike up the left splinter of the trail (north) until prominent boulders appear on the right. Several other boulders are found further up the trail as well.

*Colorado Bouldering*, Phillip Benningfield, revised 2006.
*Colorado Bouldering 2*, Benningfield and Samet, 2004.
*Colorado Front Range Bouldering: Boulder Area*, Bob Horan, 1995.

## Climbing Gyms

Boulder has three climbing gyms which provide a great escapes on a rainy day. While it rains rarely in Boulder during the summer, spring can be fairly wet. These gyms qualify amongst the premier in the country and guarantee a great experience. The Boulder Rock Club emphasizes roped climbing, while the Spot features mostly bouldering.

**The Boulder Rock Club**
2829 Mapleton Ave.
(303) 447-2804
www.boulderrock.com
Check out their ad for discounts!

**Spot Bouldering Gym**
3240 Prairie Ave.
(303) 379-8806
www.thespotgym.com

**CATS Gym**
2400 30th St.
(303) 939-9699
Gymnastics & bouldering.
Open gym on Saturday. Kids will love
to play around on the trampolines!

### Hiking
### Chautauqua Park

Chautauqua Park and its hiking opportunities beckon those who are drawn toward the Flatirons. The trail map kiosks will help you choose one of many possible loops. To reach Chautauqua head west on Baseline from Broadway to an entrance on your left just past 9th St.

### Mount Sanitas

The loop at Mount Sanitas (see Bouldering section for directions) has the added bonus of good bouldering. However, the hike itself feels longer than its three-mile length and will likely fulfill everyone's daily exercise quotient. Head west on Mapleton from Broadway to a trailhead just past 4th St.

### Eldorado Canyon / Petrified Ripple Hike

While not an "official hike" in any guide book, this pleasant walk up a closed dirt road close to Eldorado Springs leads to spectacular petrified ripple rock formations. Head west to Eldorado Springs from SH 93, head 2.4 miles and turn left at the sign for Eldorado Mountain Yoga Ashram. Park somewhere on the side before the gate bars. Parking is limited, so come early on weekends.

Walk up this gently sloping road behind the gate for half an hour to an hour to see fabulous petrified ripples (mud, with ripples or wavelets in it, that petrified under another layer of sand or mud and then became exposed) along the road. Keep walking past the first sets of ripples for even more extensive formations a bit further up the road.

Dogs are allowed but must display a City of Boulder *Voice & Sight Control* tag if off leash. You can watch the video online and pick up the tag at one of the offices.

REST DAY
ACTIVITIES

### Pearl Street Mall

This is Boulder's main attraction. How could anyone miss Pearl St. with its great food and shopping combined with jugglers, acrobats, sword swallowers, fire-eaters, and numerous other buskers in between? In one of the better acts I saw, the man mounted a very tall unicycle with a ladder and proceeded to have an assistant from below (much lower below) throw up flaming torches for him to juggle. You never quite know who will perform, or what they'll do, but you'll always find something entertaining here.

### Celestial Seasonings

4600 Sleepytime Dr., (303) 530-5300 celestialseasonings.com
These free tea factory tours, complete with gigantic spice rooms and a mesmerizing assembly line, will fascinate kids and adults alike. After the tour you can sample teas, eat in the café, or grab a cookie. Call ahead for the hour-long tour schedule du jour.

REST DAY
ACTIVITIES

### Butterfly Pavilion and Insect Center

6252 West 104th Avenue, Westminster

(303) 469-5441    www.butterflies.org

The Butterfly Pavilion will arouse every little entomologist as they peer in on beetles, centipedes and tarantulas. One of the first insect zoos, The Butterfly Pavilion shelters over 1,200 free-flying butterflies from all over the world.

### WOW! Children's Museum

110 North Harrison Ave., Lafayette

303-604-2424   www.wowmuseum.com

A combination of kid's science museum, art museum, and play learning center, WOW! lets the little ones choose among science exhibits, an arts and crafts room, a music room or a dance room. A separate toddler's room allows kids to run an electric train, mush play dough, stack blocks, or build sand castles.

OTHER
CLIMBING
GUIDES

*Serious Play: An Annotated Guide to Traditional Front Range Classics 5.2-5.9*, Steve Dieckhoff, 2002.

*Front Range Topropes*, Fred Knapp, 2000.

*Rock Climbing Colorado*, Stewart Green, 1995.

*Rock Climbing Eldorado Canyon*, Richard Rossiter, Falcon, 2000.

*Classic Boulder Climbs*, Fred Knapp and Mike Stevens, 1999.

*Rock Climbing the Flatirons*, Richard Rossiter, 1999.

*Best of Boulder Climbs*, Richard Rossiter, 1996.

*Rock Climbing Boulder Canyon*, Richard Rossiter, 1999.

*Boulder Sport Climber's Guide*, Mark Rolofson.

EMERGENCY
INFO
&
MORE

**Boulder Community Hospital- 2 Locations**

1100 Balsam Ave.

(303) 440-2273

4747 Arapahoe Ave.

(at Foothills Pkwy)

(720) 854-7000

**Boulder Chamber of Commerce**

2440 Pearl St.

(303) 442-1044

**Boulder Public Library- Main Branch**

11th Street & Arapahoe Ave.

(303) 441-3100

**George Reynolds Library**

3595 Table Mesa Dr.

(303) 441-3120

It may be easier to get online at this branch library due to generally less demand.

**Colorado Mountain School**

1-888-267-7783

www.totalclimbing.com

## ELDORADO CANYON

From Boulder, drive south on Colorado 93 to Colorado 170. Turn right on SH 170. Drive three miles to Eldorado Springs. Past town, the road turns into a potholed dirt road. Follow this to the park entrance station, pay a daily entrance fee ($6), or buy a pass. The Colorado State Parks Pass currently costs $60 and covers all Colorado State Parks.

Eldorado Canyon boasts superb face climbing on hard, sometimes polished metamorphosed sandstone. The rock in no way resembles soft desert sandstone but is more reminiscent of some quartzite. Approaches formerly ranged from about five feet to five minutes, back when they allowed parking at the base of the Bastille. To reach the climb now, walk along the road for a few hundred feet from the parking lot. My father enjoyed climbing on the Bastille when he got older since he could climb quite hard, using all four limbs, but had trouble hiking to the base of climbs with his bad hip. I climbed here both when I was pregnant and starting again when my son was two months old, since a friend could watch him nearby while we climbed.

I will describe routes on the Wind Tower and the Whale's Tail, two cliffs with very short approaches across from the Bastille. Several easy climbs are encountered here — short, one-pitch routes on the Whale's Tail and two-pitch climbs on Wind Tower. I'll also describe the mega-classic Bastille Crack and climbs on the popular practice area, Supremacy Rock. This has a very short approach and all climbs can be easily toproped.

If consulting another guide for reference, easy routes exist on the West Ridge or Rincon. However, the approach is fairly tricky to the West Ridge and fairly long to Rincon, thus I've left them out of this guide.

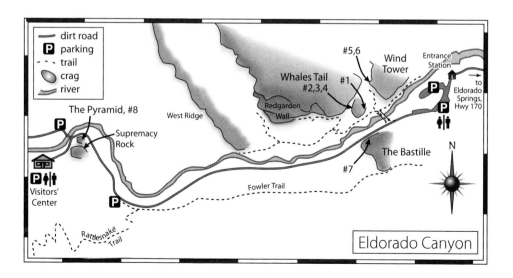

## THE WHALE'S TAIL - EAST SIDE

**Warning:**
Rockfall & other people

The east side of the Whale's Tail forms a pleasant slab, which is easy to get to, easy to climb, and perfect for introducing people to climbing. The climbing atmosphere, surrounded by the formidable sheer walls of Eldorado Canyon, is hard to beat. The climb is easy, but run-out. Small wired stoppers and #1 and #2 Camalot sized gear are indispensable. Bring long slings for the belay.

**Approach:** From the parking lot, walk up the road and cross the creek. The low-angle east face is obvious. Walk uphill along the right side of the cliff to a point about halfway up the talus on the east side.

____**1. East Slabs** 5.0–5.4 ★

I took my son up this route when he was five years old and he had a lot of fun. Two or three adults are best, so that someone can stay with the kids at the belay. Start from a point about halfway up the talus field.

**P1.** Climb up cracks and face to a tree on a good ledge to belay.

**Descent:** Traverse right from the tree to where it's easy to step directly into the gully.

**P2.** From the tree, follow a groove up to the summit.

**Descent:** Lower less experienced climbers down to the gully and then downclimb along the ridge until the gully can be reached.

Daniel Davies, visiting from Britain, goes up *West Crack* (5.2), his second-ever climb

Lauren Sigmar on West Dihedral 5.4

# THE WHALE'S TAIL - WEST SIDE

**Warning:**
Rockfall, other people, exposed ledge at base

The west face of the Whale's Tail holds three superb climbs on perfect Eldorado juggy sandstone. Nuts, cams and slings are required for this side as well.

**Approach:** After crossing the footbridge, head left along the creek to a large concrete slab. From here, head right and up a gully for 150 to 200 feet to just below some large boulders left of a ledge (see photo below). To reach the next three climbs, traverse right on a somewhat exposed ledge with one tricky move. Belay any small children across this ledge and tie them into an anchor while they are on the ledge. Scrambling across the lower ledge is easier than crossing on the upper of the two ledges

### ___2. West Crack  5.2 ★

From the large ledge below the west face, this climbs up a large obvious crack.

**P1.** This is a very easy pleasant crack with lots of face holds. It takes various sizes of nuts and cams. The anchor on top is a steel cable plus slings with rappel rings. When we last climbed this route, the slings went through the rappel rings, making the opening in the rings too tight for the rope to fit through. Toprope from this anchor with quickdraws.

**Pro**: Use all sizes of gear from small stoppers and tcus to #1 and #2 Camalots.

**Descent:** One-rope rappel to the ledge. With two ropes, lower/rappel to the ground and avoid reversing the awkward approach scramble.

Whale's Tail - West

### ___3. West Dihedral  5.4 ★

This route follows the large dihedral about 10 to 20 feet right of *West Crack*.

**P1.** Pleasant climbing with laybacking, stemming, and face holds. An anchor at the top of this corner consists of slings with rappel rings. I backed it up with a cam to toprope.

**Pro**: Use all sizes of gear from small stoppers and tcus to #1 and #2 Camalots.

**Descent:** Traverse left to the anchor for *West Crack* to rappel.

### ___4. Center Face  5.6 R

While up here, with a toprope set up, it's possible to also climb the face between *West Crack* and *West Dihedral*. Various alternative routes abound, all somewhat lacking in potential gear placements, so choose between soloing or toproping this climb. It provides an opportunity for superb face climbing at a reasonable grade, and the more adventurous may enjoy the chance to climb a slightly harder route.

# WIND TOWER

The Wind Tower is large enough that the routes are multi-pitch, so your party will get some practice at organizing belays, and everyone in your party must be comfortable being high above the ground. The descent involves a traverse along a ledge after pitch 2; kids should be on belay. There is potential rockfall hazard here, from other parties above. It's best to schedule midweek visits as the Wind Tower can be crowded on weekends. On the plus side, the climbs are superb and the views tremendous.

**Approach:** Cross the footbridge. The gully between the Whale's Tail and the Wind Tower will be directly ahead. Hike north up the gully (the Wind Tower trail with stone steps) to reach the west face. *Wind Ridge* goes up the crack just left of the arête separating the south and west faces. *Breezy* ascends a corner left of Wind Ridge.

____**5. Breezy** 5.4 ★★★

*Breezy* combines crack, face, and stemming moves on excellent rock.

**P1.** There are various starts to the climb, however my preferred method is to go around the arête from the base of *Wind Ridge* and step out on the face on good holds. We tried another start which lies about 40 feet left of *Wind Ridge* where a fixed pin marks the route. Here you will find an obvious corner that takes you to the *Breezy* dihedral. However, this start seemed more difficult that 5.4.

From here, climb up to join *Wind Ridge* and then traverse left into the corner forming the *Breezy* dihedral. From here on, follow the obvious corner to a ledge with a tree. Belay here if your second is not very confident, since it's possible to still communicate well from this ledge.

**P2.** From here, follow a delightful crack on the face left of the corner to the ledge system forming the walk off from the south face routes.

**Descent:** Walk left and scramble down the ledge to the Wind Ridge trail. Follow this to the base of your climb.

### 6. Wind Ridge 5.6 ★★★

I've heard people call *Wind Ridge* the best 5.6 in Eldorado Canyon, and others say it's the best 5.6 in Colorado. In either case, it's definitely a route worth climbing. With that reputation, many people think it's worth doing, so try to come here early on a weekday. Two benefits are derived from this plan: availability and comfortable temps in the shade.

*Wind Ridge* is a multi-pitch climb, so take a second who's comfortable on their own, or climb in a party of three. Try any one of three different starts for *Wind Ridge*. Whichever way you go, the start is the hardest part of the climb. Start on a nice ledge, just left of the arête proper, and below an overhang with a right-facing flake going through it. Three starting options are given below.

**P1a.** Start by going diagonally up left on balancy face holds, bypassing the right-facing flake, to a horizontal band of jugs. Traverse right, move around the corner, and finally step onto the arête/face.

**P1b.** Alternatively, go straight up the layback crack in the face, which provides the most challenging start at 5.8.

**P1c.** Finally, it's possible to climb up to the right-facing layback crack, stem right onto the arête, and step around the corner onto the main face.

Whatever your chosen start may be, use long runners to protect the second so that they have a rope from above, not sideways (and to reduce potential rope drag). Once on the main face, pleasant climbing continues up to a ledge. Here, several people can sit comfortably on an incut ledge. The anchor right at the ledge is minimal, so I anchor here and on the crack that continues up the face as well.

**P2.** The second pitch is longer and it's hard to see the second climber following from the top of the pitch. From the ledge, traverse right slightly and head up a dogleg crack to a chimney section above. Though intimidating for non-crack climbers, it is much easier than it appears and well equipped with face holds on both sides. Continue up cracks to a bigger ledge strewn with some loose rock, and belay. Be careful here not to knock any rock down on climbers below.

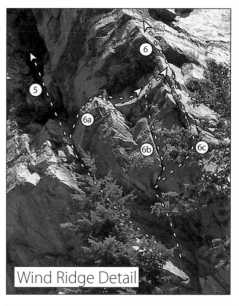

Wind Ridge Detail

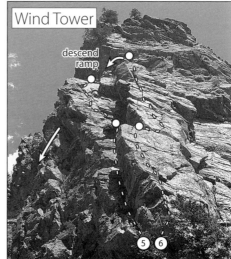

Wind Tower

**Descent:** It is best to traverse off left from the top of pitch 2, and down a ramp. There is a third pitch above, which starts with a pumpy roof followed by scrambling on easy terrain. The descent from the top of the third pitch is very tricky.

To descend from the top of the second pitch, traverse left on the ledge until it widens. Belay any children, beginners, and shaky or less confident seconds around the corner on the first part of this ledge. It narrows down just past the belay stance and provides noticeable exposure. After the beginning, the ramp widens and the exposure decreases. Use your judgment as to when to remove the belay. After some more scrambling down the ramp, the gully joins the trail, which quickly leads directly to the start of the climb.

Tristan Hechtel halfway up pitch one

## THE BASTILLE

Some years ago, when fewer people climbed and we enjoyed less traffic, one could literally park at the base of the Bastille and belay from your car bumper. Today cars continually cruise up and down the road past the Bastille, making the climbing experience somewhat different. Try to climb here early on a weekday... less picnic traffic and shorter lines for this classic line.

### ___7. Bastille Crack, pitch 1, 5.8 ★

Some climbers have said that they came to Eldorado Canyon with one goal: to climb the *Bastille Crack*. While the climb may be a little challenging for the complete beginner, most children with some climbing experience can climb the first pitch. Older climbers will also enjoy the first pitch due to its very short and flat approach and the easy descent – just lower off the anchors.

From the parking lot, walk up the road to the Bastille on your left. Take a number, wait your turn, and watch the climbers in front for beta.

Start to the right of the obvious crack and climb up face holds to a flake. Small gear (yellow TCU or alien) fits in at the flake. From here, traverse left to the crack. Good stoppers fit low in the crack before committing to the move across. For a crack climber, it's a straightforward move. I've seen people struggle here, doing everything they can to try, gain height while avoiding a hand jam in the crack. With jamming, climbing the crack becomes a lot easier.

It's possible to toprope the climb from a good anchor with chains atop the first pitch. For extra training, if no one is in line waiting to get on the Bastille, toprope the crack to the left, the 5.10+ *Northcutt Start*.

## SUPREMACY ROCK (THE PYRAMID)

**Warning:** Expertise in the toprope setup is essential to safety

Drive up towards the parking for Rincon and the picnic area. Walk across the bridge and 30 feet up and right to the base of the pyramid, the smaller buttress right beside the road.

**___8. Simple Simon Slab** 5.6 R ★

To set up a toprope, walk to the right of the cliff toward a large tree behind the cliff and ascend the easier gully going to the second tree on the right. Either bring several very long runners (over 20 feet) to sling the tree behind the pyramid or bring a second rope to tie off the tree. Run the slings through a notch at the top of the pyramid that acts as a directional.

*Simple Simon* has a flat base area, very short approach, and a pleasant, low-angle slab with some cracks. The rock here is a very polished gneiss, quite different from the Eldorado Fountain sandstone.

The R-rating obviously applies to *leading* this short route. Climb the crack up the middle of the Pyramid's north face. Try several variations here – go right more, or left of the crack, to make it more challenging.

## The Thumbs Up and Thumbs Down on Boulder Canyon...............

 **Pros:** Classic climbing area; short approaches; free; easy access to Boulder with many activities; some easy routes

 **Cons:** No nearby camping; crowded on weekends; potential rockfall

## Climbing here is mostly...

## Logistics at a Glance .................................................................

? time
Approach

0 to 10 minutes, Older or disabled climbers will have an easy approach at Castle Rock.

Food?

Boulder has lots of restaurants, of all kinds. The closest are downtown in the Pearl Street area.

Rock Type

Granite

Cell Coverage

Not up the canyon

Climb Type

Some sport and some gear. In addition to a rope and draws, it's wise to pack a cam or two, perhaps some nuts even at sport cliffs.

Hot Spots

No wireless internet in the canyon, but many places in Boulder.

Ages

Any Age
Best 7 or older

Dogs?

Yes

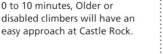

Camping?

Nearest campground is small, and in Boulder Canyon. Otherwise Golden Gate Campground. See Camping text for more details.

Seasons

Spring, Summer and Fall are best.

# BOULDER CANYON

Many crags line the canyon on both sides of the road. Of these, Castle Rock provides by far the most child-and-grandparent or wheelchair-friendly access. Drive to within a few feet of the beginning of the routes and park in a large flat dirt road that circles the south side of Castle Rock. I've seen kids parked here in strollers while their parents climb.

The Sport Park contains more moderate sport climbs than any other crag in the canyon. The trails are maintained and the base areas mostly flat. The major obstacle here is definitely Boulder Creek. During the spring run off the crossing is treacherous and requires a Tyrolean traverse. A Tyrolean crossing would be difficult for anyone under 12 or 13. During other times of the year an ankle-deep wade may still be necessary.

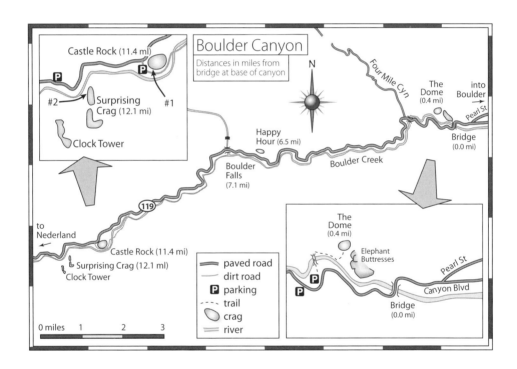

Ariel and Brian Doub enjoy a day at Castle Rock. Ariel climbs *West Face* 5.5 at right.

## CASTLE ROCK

**Warning:**
Rockfall

From downtown Boulder take Broadway to Canyon. Turn west on Canyon, reset the odometer at the bridge (Arapahoe merges with Canyon), and drive uphill for 11.4 miles (mile marker 29.3) to a large cliff on the left – Castle Rock. Turn left and park anywhere along the base of the cliff. Walk about 20 feet to reach the base of some climbs. There isn't a much shorter approach than this! The easier climbs are on the west side of Castle Rock, the first side you drive by when you turn left to park.

### ___1. West Face 5.5 ★

Two pine trees sit atop a ledge about 75 feet up. A large chimney and crack leads up from the ground to the left-hand pine tree, below which are two bolts with rings. There are various possible routes up: climb either in the large chimney, slightly to the left of the chimney (perhaps the easiest option), or to the right of the chimney. Higher up, the chimney turns into more of a gully with some large chockstones and blocks to surmount. While the climbing is generally easy, reaching around and above the blocks can be tricky for smaller children.

Once the toprope is set up, have people try different options. They can climb up left of the chimney on their first time, then if they do well they can try the chimney itself and practice chimney technique, and then if that goes well they can try the right side of the chimney. The climb gives full value: three climbs for the price of one set of anchors!

Climbers may encounter some loose rock. While the climb is easy, a new leader may feel nervous about leading since he will need to place gear. To descend, lower off the anchor bolts. It's not the easiest lower-off, since one has to go over some blocks and down past a chimney. For children who have lowered off very little, they may find it intimidating since it's not the easiest descent. If there are three climbers,

one could rappel beside them to offer advice and support. Alternatively, continue up another pitch and walk off the top.

**Descent:** From the summit, head north and scramble down ramps and ledges down the back (north) side.

Castle Rock

Ariel Doub on *West Face*

## SPORT PARK

**Warning:**
Possible high
water creek
crossing

About 12.1 miles from downtown (0.7 miles past Castle Rock), is the Boulder Sport Park, which includes Surprising Crag, Clock Tower, and several others. I will describe climbs on Surprising Crag, which has several easy routes, and on the Clock Tower.

Park at either the first pullout on the left, or pass it to park at a large pullout on the right. From the first pullout, cross the creek to a trail. The creek is quite low in late summer and early fall, an ideal time to climb here. In spring the water can be much higher (knee to mid-thigh on me) and may not be a good place to take kids, older people, or novice climbers that tend towards timidness. In September, the water was about six inches deep at the most and crossing the creek proved quite easy. I usually bring sandals for crossing the creek, as I don't like walking barefoot on the rocks on the bottom. Children may want help crossing on the smooth, rounded, slippery rocks on the creek bottom.

On the other side, a fairly wide trail leads straight and slightly uphill and crosses an old aqueduct trail. Continue more or less straight uphill to the south face of Surprising Crag ahead. Head slightly left towards the crag. A large flat sunny area welcomes climbers to the base of Surprising Crag. From here, several routes beckon.

**\_\_\_2. Choss Temple Pilots** 5.8 ★★
On the south face of Surprising Crag there are three bolted face climbs. The left most is 5.8 and the two to the right, which go over the small roof, are both 5.11. *Choss Temple Pilots* ascends on decent rock along a well-bolted line. The anchor bolts have rings, to simplify toproping and descents. Bear left at the second bolt - don't get deceived into heading right toward the roof and the 5.11s! 6 clips.

### ___3. Chasing Sticks 5.9+ ★

Directly to the right of the wall with the previous three climbs is a large chimney. The wall to the right hosts numerous bolted crack climbs that allow one to practice crack technique while enjoying bolted protection. 5 clips.

### ___4. Dutch Oven 5.9+

The first of the bolted routes right of the chimney, *Chasing Sticks*, is a bit harder than *Choss Temple Pilots*. Try the further right cracks instead. The second and third cracks both go at 5.10, but the 4th crack, at 5.9, is the easiest of the lot. Some climbers may stick clip the first bolt. I led it without a stick clip, and found it reasonable, but the initial rock is a bit chossy. 6 clips.

### ___5. Monkey Bob 5.8 ★★

Starting around to the right of the arête, *Monkey Bob* allows a fun romp up the cliff. The first bolt is visible from the south side and then the route heads around to the other side. 4 clips.

### ___6. The Touch 5.8 ★★

Walk further right around the corner. Pass two hard (5.11) bolted face climbs and come to two cracks that start in a corner. *The Touch* provides excellent climbing with a choice of using either the crack or avoiding it and climbing on the face. 6 clips.

### ____7. Frictionary 5.7 ★★★

Continue right from *The Touch* around the next arête. Start right of the arête up this somewhat spicy 5.7. The start is easier if one traverses in from the right, so I set the climb up to toprope and leave the bottom bolt unclipped. For climbers who don't want to lead it, walk around to the top of this route to set up a toprope. 6 clips.

Courtney on *Chicken Delight* 5.10c

# sherpani

breathe | *give* | stretch | | go

**Sherpani**

Definition
: A Nepalase term
used for a female
Sherpa; a member of a Tibetan people living on the high southern
slopes of the Himalayas, who serve as expert guides on Himalayan
mountaineering expeditions.

## sherpani || for baby

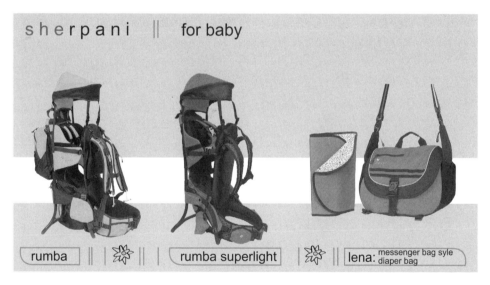

rumba || || rumba superlight || || lena: messenger bag syle / diaper bag

## sherpani || for women

For more information on Sherpani products visit us at **www.sherpani-bags.com**

## CLOCK TOWER / CHICKEN WALL

**Warning:**
Possible high
water creek
crossing

From Surprising Crag hike south toward the Clock Tower, a prominent crag you can see easily from Surprising Crag. The wall on the lower left side, the Chicken Wall, sports a number of nice face routes.

____**8. Weasel in the Chicken Coop** 5.9 ★★★
Head for the route that is the farthest right route on the Chicken Wall which starts by 2 huge bolts. The climbing provides easy clips from good stances and nice moves on interesting rock. The start is easier if one traverses in from the right. Climb to the left and right of the bolts to reach the best holds. 5 clips.

____**9. Chicken Delight** 5.10c
Another climb...as long as you're in the vicinity. Follow the wall uphill (left) to the last set of bolts. Climb the face with pockets and crimpers and use the arête as necessary. 7 clips.

## THE DOME AND THE ELEPHANT BUTTRESSES

*While there are a number of easy routes here, access remains a bit tricky. To reach the Elephant Buttresses head 0.4 miles up Boulder Canyon past the intersection at Arapahoe. Walk from your car across the bridge to the water pipe. Here begins the difficulty. Balance along the water pipe, and even belay from the top of the pipe for some routes. It's a wide pipe, and certainly comfortable for adult climbers, but I wouldn't want to take small children across, nor is there a spacious area near the base where they can play. Older climbers may have balance concerns, but since the pipe is essentially flat, an approach here may be easy for them. This solves half the equation - reaching the base. After reaching the top, the standard descent involves scrambling off the back and down the slope between The Dome and The First Elephant Buttress. We took my son up the two-pitch Standard Route on the Third Elephant Buttress when he was seven years old, and comfortable on the pipe, the scramble down, and on the belay stance halfway up the climb. People who can handle tricky approaches, scrambling down loose descents, and multi-pitch climbs, can enjoy various routes here. However, those climbs are somewhat beyond the scope of this book - which after all, focuses on short, or at least relatively flat approaches, safe base areas, and reasonable descents.*

## HAPPY HOUR CRAG

*Happy Hour Crag presents a similar situation to the Elephant Buttresses. The trail to the base is steep and loose, the base area itself is not flat, and the descent off the top is loose. However, some pleasant moderate climbs exist here. One of the more comprehensive guidebooks describes the climbs at both of these areas in greater detail.*

Lauren Sigman on **Peaches And Scream** 5.7

# CASTLEWOOD CANYON

When visiting Denver, Castlewood Canyon provides a good place to start on short, close-in climbing while getting used to the altitude. It's a short drive from Denver (between one half hour to 45 minutes, depending on traffic), has short approaches (about five minutes) and most of the routes can be toproped. Fred Knapp, in his book *Front Range Topropes*, calls it possibly the best toproping area in the Front Range. Easy access to toprope anchors make this a family gem, but there's enough quality sport climbing to round out the program. The canyon provides some of the best cool-weather bouldering in Colorado and offers a viable and less-crowded alternative to Shelf Road.

While approaches to the cliffs are short, the trail rises steeply, often ascending stone or wood steps, which may be difficult for older or handicapped climbers. The base areas by the cliff teem with flat boulders to sit on, shady trees to play beneath and some sandy spots for the kids. For people taking kids climbing, Castlewood Canyon offers many advantages. It's possible to scramble to the top, set up several topropes and belay from the ground.

Castlewood Canyon is a great place to take visiting parents. While taking pictures, two climbers asked me what I was taking photos for. When I told them about the book, both said that they had brought their fathers here to climb and asked me about other areas I would recommend.

Castlewood Canyon's proximity to the Denver metro area offers close-by shopping (about five minutes from Franktown), lodging in Castle Rock or Denver, numerous fun activities and great dining.

This guide describes the Grocery Store Wall, perhaps the best toproping cliff at Castlewood Canyon — offering many bolted anchors, a dense concentration of fun climbs, a meager approach and straightforward access to the clifftop.

The Lucas Homestead Historic Site

## The Thumbs Up and Thumbs Down on Castlewood Canyon........

 **Pros:** Very short approach; good toproping area; warm in winter; easy access from Denver; close to Frank-town for groceries and supplies.

 **Cons:** Climbs are very short; fewer leads than topropes; hot in summer; poison ivy; rattlesnakes; park fee $5 a day (a Colorado State Parks Pass for $60 covers all Colorado State Parks); no camping.

## Climbing here is mostly...

## Logistics at a Glance

**? time**
Approach

5-10 min
steep at times

Rock Type

Castlewood
Conglomerate Sandstone

Climb Type

Gear for Toproping
Rope, slings, biners for most climbs, cams for some toprope anchors.

Ages

All Ages at Base,
Stairs and steps challenging for older/disabled climbers.

Camping?

No camping in the park.

Food?

Castle Rock and Franktown are super close. Denver metro area in general.

Cell Coverage

Yes

Hot Spots

No wireless internet in canyon.

Dogs?

Yes, on leash

Seasons

Fall through Spring Best;
Summer can be hot.

## How many routes are at the Grocery Store Wall?*

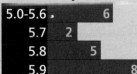

| Grade | Routes |
|---|---|
| 5.0-5.6 | 6 |
| 5.7 | 2 |
| 5.8 | 5 |
| 5.9 | 8 |

* This statistic is for reference only, not all climbs of these grades have been chosen for this book.

**From Denver:** Take I-25 south to Exit 184 (by the Castle Rock Outlet Stores). Take a left and go east on Founder's Parkway about 4.0 miles to Highway 86. Turn left (East) and follow Highway 86 for 4.5 miles to a sign for Castlewood Canyon Road. The sign comes up suddenly and is hard to see. If you cross the bridge over Cherry Creek, you've gone too far. Turn right and follow Castlewood Canyon Road for 2.1 miles to the kiosk at the park's west entrance. Drive a gravel road another 0.6 miles to the first parking lot on the right.

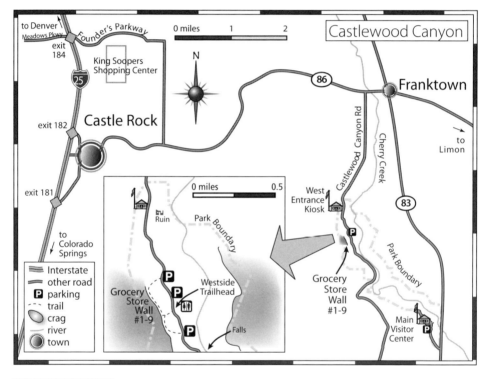

SETTING UP
CAMP

1. **Devil's Head Campground**. This is the closest camping, about 15 miles west of Sedalia. From the King Soopers shopping area on Founder's Pkwy, head west on Founder's, cross over I-25, and continue straight. Founder's becomes Meadows Pkwy. Take a right onto US-85N for 5 miles, then turn left onto CO 67 at Sedalia. Drive about ten miles west on Highway 67 to Rampart Range Road. Turn left (south) on Rampart Range Road for about 8.5 miles.

2. **Indian Creek Equestrian Camp**, 19316 Goddard Ranch Ct., Morrison, CO 80465         www.reserveamerica.com
Sites here are both first-come, first-served sites as well as by reservation.

HOTELS &
MOTELS

**Best Western Inn and Suites**, 595 Genoa Way, (877) 574-2464
Clean, quiet, and close to loads of restaurants, this hotel complete with a
pool and free internet is sure to please everybody...even the family dog can
come along.

**Hampton Inn Castle Rock**, 4830 Castleton Way, (303) 660-9800
Service and extreme cleanliness separate this hotel from the rest. Great
pool area!

SHOPPING &
GROCERIES

**Safeway**, 880 S. Perry St., Castle Rock, (303) 688-5028

**King Soopers**, 100 Founders Pkwy., Castle Rock, (303) 663-0177

**Outlets at Castle Rock**, 5050 Factory Shops Blvd., Castle Rock

**Rocky Mountain Harley-Davidson**, 970 Park St., Castle Rock,
(303) 327-7799

RESTAURANTS
& COFFEE

Castle Rock has many fast food and chain restaurants — and a nice
brewpub. For a real treat for the friends or family, you'll need to head into
Denver, where the dining choices are fantastic. Kyle Wagner, *The Denver
Post* dining critic, recommends a selection of reasonably priced places in
Denver. Below are some of my favorites:

## Castle Rock

**Rockyard Brewing Company**,
880 W. Castleton Rd., Castle Rock, (303) 814-9273
OK, the parents and grandparents deserve a treat now and then too. This
brew pub is in Castle Rock, so you don't need to wrestle with Denver traffic to get there.

**Castle Rock Bar and Grill**, 302 Wilcox St., (303) 660-3814

**Coffee Lodge**, 102 S. Wilcox Street, (303) 660-1215

## Denver

**Cherry Creek Grill**, 184 Steele St, Denver, (303) 322-3524
Wagner lists this as his kid's top pick. With their banana cream pie and
Oreo cookies ice cream sandwiches, I can see why!

**Domo Restaurant**, 1365 Osage Street, Denver, (303) 595-3666
I really like Japanese food and it's hard to find good fare that's not expensive. Domo, a casual Japanese restaurant, provides good food with a
comfortable and interesting interior.

**Luca d'Italia**, 711 Grant, Denver, (303) 832-6600
This is a nice Italian restaurant.

**Mezcal**, 3230 E. Colfax Ave., Denver, (303) 322-5219
Mexican cuisine.

# What Else Can We Do That's Fun?

BOULDERING

## Bouldering

When we last climbed at Castlewood, I saw almost as many climbers walking around with large crash pads on their back as I saw climbers on topropes on the cliff. Considering that the cliffs are only about 50 feet high in places, it makes sense to get a workout on several 10 – 20 foot boulder problems! Climbers who enjoy conglomerate (resembling Maple Canyon) should like bouldering here.

Benningfield devotes 20 pages of *Colorado Bouldering* to Castlewood Canyon as does Horan in his book. (See other climbing guides section).

REST DAY
ACTIVITIES

## Climbing Gyms

Denver boasts several excellent gyms, as does nearby Boulder. For climbers in Denver for a business meeting, the gym could be a good way to find potential climbing partners.

| Paradise Rock Gym | Rock'n & Jam'n | Rock'n & Jam'n |
|---|---|---|
| 6260 N. Washington Street, Unit 5, Denver | 9499 N. Washington St., Unit C, Thornton | 7390 S. Fraser Street, #E Centennial |
| (303) 286-8168 | (303) 254-6299 | (303) 254-6299 |
| www.paradiserock.com | www.rocknandjamn.com | www.rocknandjamn.com |

Onward

## Hiking
### Castlewood Canyon State Park
### The Lucas Homestead Historic Site
Castlewood Canyon offers myriad short hiking trails, some meandering through the micro-canyons along Cherry Creek and others skirting the cliff tops. Horses, wheelchairs, and bikes are permitted on some trails within the park. Other trails visit historic sites, such as the ruins of the Castlewood Dam (about 1890) and the Lucas Homestead Historic Site.
www.parks.state.co.us

### Devil's Head Trail and Lookout Tower
This forested, lush hike begins in the picnic area adjacent to Devil's Head Campground and ends at the last fire lookout for the Pike National Forest.
www.douglas.co.us/community/historic/Devil's_Head_Lookout.html

REST DAY
ACTIVITIES

## Other Attractions

### Six Flags Elitch Gardens

2000 Elitche Cir., Denver

(303) 595-4386    www.elitchgardens.com

Kids flock to this downtown summer fun hub. With over 45 rides and the Island Kingdom Water Park, there's entertainment for the littlest ones, older kids, and teens.

### Water World

88th Ave. and Pecos St., Denver    www.waterworldcolorado.com

Water World, about 15 minutes north of Denver, is one of America's largest waterparks. When temperatures rise, playing here might be more fun than sweating on the cliffs, even for parents. My son's favorite rides include Voyage to the Center of the Earth and the Zoomerang. In the Voyage, you ride an inner tube down an underground river past exciting Jurassic animals and scenes. To slide on the Zoomerang, kids must be at least 42 inches tall.

### Denver Zoo

2600 Steele St., Denver    www.denverzoo.org

Who doesn't love a zoo? If it gets too hot to climb, cool off watching the polar bears. If you have a rainy day (luckily not too many of those in Colorado), you can tour Tropical Discovery, a 45-foot-tall glass pyramid enclosing a rain forest.

### Denver Mint

320 West Colfax Avenue, Denver

United States Mint  www.usmint.gov/mint_tours

Tour the Mint; see how our money is made.

MUSEUMS

### Denver Museum of Nature and Science

2001 Colorado Boulevard, Denver    www.dmns.org

An Imax, the plantarium, special exhibits, and interactive displays will broaden the mind while the body recovers from yesterday's climbing.

### The Children's Museum of Denver

2121 Children's Museum Drive, Denver    www.cmdenver.org

(off I-25 and 23rd Avenue)

Enjoy a hands on experience designed for kids under 9. Located downtown, super close to Elitch's.

OTHER
CLIMBING
GUIDES

*Front Range Topropes*, Fred Knapp, 2000.

*Rock Climbing Colorado*, Stewart Green, 1995.

*A Rock Climber's Guide to Castlewood Canyon State Park, Colorado*, Thomas Hanson.

EMERGENCY
INFO
&
MORE

**Swedish Medical Center**

501 E. Hampden Ave.

Englewood, CO

(303) 788-5000

**Castle Rock
Chamber of Commerce**

420 Jerry St.

Castle Rock, CO

(303) 688-4597

**Littleton Hospital Urgent Care**

7730 S. Broadway

Littleton, CO

(303) 730-5895

**Denver Public Library**

10 W. Fourteenth Ave. Pkwy.

Denver, CO

(720) 865-1111

www.denverlibrary.org

# THE GROCERY STORE WALL

**Approach:** From the west entrance, drive 0.6 miles to the first parking lot on the right and look for a sign, "Climber's Trail." Follow the trail uphill for five to ten minutes to the base of the wall. The trail hits the Grocery Store Wall near a large right-facing corner with a right-leaning, right-facing flake that forms a roof. The first climb described, *Peaches and Scream* is directly to the right of the corner.

The routes at Grocery Store Wall are vertical, and sometimes poorly-protected leads. But they make great topropes, and are described as such in the text. To access the clifftop for toprope prep, walk left to an easy chimney system and scramble up (or walk further left for an even easier option). Once at the top, walk right to find the bolt anchors above the routes.

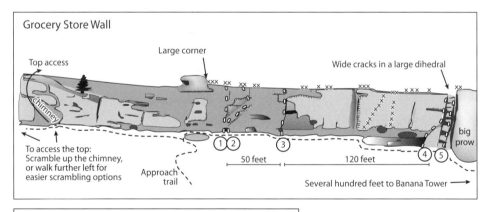

## Routes Featured
1. Peaches and Scream 5.7
2. Zucchini 5.5
3. Rat's Nest 5.9
4. Carmel Corner 5.5
5. Carmel Corner Layback 5.5

### ___1. Peaches and Scream 5.7 ★★

Look for the obvious large right-facing corner with a big roof near the top and a right-leaning, right facing flake to the right of the corner. Face climb up to a left-facing flake (see photo to right) and lieback up the flake. Continue up face holds toward the anchor.

**Descent:** The last person will need to scramble back down the chimney you climbed up to set up the toprope.

**Additional Gear/Anchor Suggestion:** At the top, about 20 feet right of the large corner, a bolt anchor with chains allows toproping both *Peaches and Scream* and the route just left, *Zucchini*.

### ___2. Zucchini 5.5

Start at the same place as for *Peaches and Scream*. Climb up a few feet, then head right along the right-angling crack (seam) and corner.

**Descent:** See descent for *Peaches and Scream*.

**Additional Gear Suggestion:** It may be best to place a directional anchor for novice climbers toproping the route. See anchor suggestion for *Peaches and Scream*.

**Peaches and Scream** goes up to the left-facing flake above the climber. **Zucchini** follows the right-angling seam and crack to the right of the climber.

### ___3. Rat's Nest 5.9 ★★

To find this climb, walk about 50 feet right from *Zucchini* to a thin crack/seam that goes up to a large hole.

The bouldery start can be tamed by standing on the dead stump at the start. Apparently, at the time of the first ascent, the stump was taller allowing climbers to reach the hole. Thus, don't hesitate to give friends a boost to reach the hole if necessary. From the hole, follow the crack toward the top.

**Descent:** The anchor bolts at the top have no chains or rappel rings, so you can't rappel from here. One person needs to climb to the top, remove the draws, then walk off.

**Additional Gear Suggestion:** Bring your own slings or quickdraws for setting up your toprope from the bolt anchor.

# Carmel Corner Area

Walk about 120 feet right from Rat's Nest to locate a very large left-facing dihedral. There are two nice routes here. *Carmel Corner* takes a dihedral system just left of the corner; while *Carmel Corner Layback* follows the wide cracks in the dihedral direct. The base is picnic friendly — flat with big shade trees. *Blood Pudding*, which can also be set up as a toprope, could also provide a good challenge.

### ___4. Carmel Corner 5.5 ★

Start under flakes and ledges just left of the main corner. Face climb or stem up these flakes and ledges and head toward the anchor.

**Descent:** One person needs to climb to the top, remove the gear, then walk off.

**Additional Gear Suggestion:** For toproping, there are two places to anchor at the top of the dihedral. The anchor directly above *Carmel Corner* consists of only one bolt. A large cam, such as a #2 or #3 Camalot fits next to the bolt. Since the route lies just left of the corner, it may help to place gear for directionals.

### ___5. Carmel Corner Layback 5.5 ★

The bottom is pretty easy but the top gets a little trickier. Jam or stem the large corner crack. Near the top, either layback or chimney the left-hand of the two cracks.

**Descent:** There are anchor bolts at the top for toproping, but the bolts have no chains or rappel rings, so you can't rappel from here. One person needs to climb to the top, remove the draws, then walk off.

**Additional Gear Suggestion:** See *Carmel Corner* for details.

### ___5a. Blood Pudding 5.9+

At the top you may notice a pair of bolts right of the single bolt anchor at the top of *Carmel Corner*. This anchor provides a toprope for a 5.9+ face climb, *Blood Pudding*, on the wall right of the corner.

**Additional Gear Suggestion:** This anchor lacks chains or rappel rings; bring draws.

**Descent:** One person needs to climb to the top, remove the gear, then walk off.

Carmel Corner Area

Tristan Hechtel on *Carmel Corner Layback* 5.5

# Banana Tower

To reach the bottom of Banana Tower, walk right along a climber's trail for several hundred feet to an obvious detached tower in front of the main wall.

Reaching the top of Banana Tower can be a bit tricky. Access the top as for the previous routes, or another option is to walk north (right) along the base past the climbs to where it is easy to hike up. Walk along the cliff top to the detached pillar forming Banana Tower. Step across the gap (about three feet) to reach the top. Here, 3 bolts provide anchors for several climbs up the tower. The bolts lack rappel rings, so after toproping climbs on Banana Tower repeat the step-across to retrieve the quickdraws.

### ___6. Banana Split Chimney 5.4

Located between the main wall and Banana Tower, the rock in the chimney is fairly coarse, so consider wearing kneepads, long pants, and a long-sleeved shirt. A flake in the north side makes the ascent a bit easier.

**Descent:** Walk and scramble down the right side of the cliff, about five minutes. The approach at the right (north) end of the cliff is easier than the approach up the gully/chimney on the left side. We climbed up the left approach, climbed routes from left (south) to right (north) and descended down the right side.

### ___7. Banana Peel 5.8 ★★

Follow face holds and discontinuous cracks up the left side of Banana Tower's east face.
**Descent:** *See Banana Split Chimney.*

### ___8. Banana Shake 5.9 ★★

Follow face holds up the right side of the east face of Banana Tower, which is harder since it avoids the large, obvious holds.
**Descent:** *See Banana Split Chimney.*

### ___9. Banana Flip 5.6

Ascend the north ridge of Banana Tower, placing directionals on the traverses. It may be easier to belay from the top of the tower.
**Descent:** *See Banana Split Chimney.*

Banana Tower sits in front of the main wall

#9 follows north ridge of tower

Climber on Classic Dihedral 5.7+

# ELEVENMILE CANYON & THE SOUTH PLATTE

If afternoon thunderstorms near Rocky Mountain National Park and Lumpy Ridge deter you from climbing there, look for better, more accessible cracks at Turkey Rocks. The South Platte's lower altitude allows one to enjoy warmer temperatures and somewhat dryer weather than in Estes Park. For climbers who couldn't reserve a campsite near Rocky Mountain National Park, select among numerous sites in Elevenmile Canyon and primitive camping at Turkey Rocks. Both the climbs and the camping are less crowded than climbs in popular areas of Rocky Mountain National Park. Lush riparian meadows border the South Platte River allowing opportunities for fishing or boating in nearby Elevenmile State Park.

The South Platte covers a vast area ranging from Pine Junction at Highway 285 in the north, down Highway 67 towards Deckers and Westcreek along the southeast edge, to Elevenmile Canyon, just south of Lake George on Highway 24 at the southern end. Small roadside crags with one pitch climbs sit next to large granite towers and domes offering longer routes. Elevenmile Canyon meanders along the South Platte River and offers some of the nicest camping in the state. In fall, gold and orange aspen surround white cliffs and climbers can enjoy warm sunny days into early October (but cool nights).

The rock consists primarily of the same granite as the Pikes Peak batholith, forming both smooth Yosemite-like cracks and holdless slabs reminiscent of Tuolomne Meadows. Several climbers train at Turkey Rocks in spring and then head to Yosemite to polish off hard testpieces there. However, for climbers bringing their family here on summer vacation, they're probably more interested in teaching them to climb easier cracks. One can find plenty here, particularly at Elevenmile Canyon, Bucksnort Slab, Sphinx Rock and Turkey Rocks.

The Platte generally has cooler weather than Unaweep, on the Western slope, and thus provides a good option for climbing in summer. I've enjoyed warm sunny days climbing there on south-facing cliffs in March or October.

I'll separately describe the climbs in Elevenmile Canyon and the rest of the South Platte since one camps in different campgrounds to climb at the two areas (actually, camp in different places depending on which cliff you wish to climb in the South Platte!) and approaches them on different roads. However, they share similar rock, environment, amenities and other activities, so I'll describe the latter jointly for both areas.

# ELEVENMILE CANYON

Elevenmile Canyon provides some of the most beautiful camping in Colorado. Stay in any one of six campgrounds along the South Platte River as it winds through the canyon. The Forest Service supplies flat campsites, picnic tables, fire grates, water, pit toilets, and garbage cans among beautiful scenery beside the river. Walk to the climbs from Spillway or Cove campground. Beside Spillway campground, a gently sloping trail winds up the hillside to good views of the river valley. A sign says, "Scenic Overlook, 1/2 mile". When I hiked it one October morning, rabbits grazed along the trail up the hill. Campsites are by reservation and over Memorial Day every site in every campground was reserved.

Approaches are short: belay some climbs tied in to the car bumper. Not all approaches are this short but several trails to the cliff are fairly flat. Elevenmile Canyon has some of the best beginner and moderate routes in the area on Elevenmile Dome and Arch Rock. Elevenmile Dome has a very short approach - one of the routes starts literally three feet from the car. Arch Rock has a slightly longer approach but easy short routes that make it well worth the hike up to the cliff.

Arch Rock

## The Thumbs Up and Thumbs Down on Elevenmile

 **Pros:** Some very short approaches; beautiful scenery; great camping with gorgeous fall colors; quality crack climbing on good rock; easy climbs; river.

 **Cons:** Dirt road; remote; few nearby amenities; fee area.

### Climbing here is mostly...

## Logistics at a Glance

 Approach — 1 minute flat to 10 minutes uphill depending on the crag.

 Food? — Lake George or drive to nearby Florissant.

  Rock Type — Granite

 Cell Coverage — No

  Climb Type — 2 Ropes, nuts, stoppers, cams. Kneepads to climb a chimney.

 Hot Spots — No

 Ages — Any age

 Dogs? — Yes

 Camping? — Several USFS campgrounds, $10.00 a night. More details in setting up camp.

 Seasons — Spring, Summer or Fall

## How many routes are routes are here?*

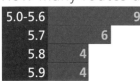

| Grade | Count |
|---|---|
| 5.0-5.6 | 9 |
| 5.7 | 6 |
| 5.8 | 4 |
| 5.9 | 4 |

* This statistic is for reference only, not all climbs of these grades have been chosen for this book.

GETTING
THERE

Take Highway 24 to Lake George. By Starky's General Store, look for a sign that says "National Forest Access: 11 Mile Canyon Recreation Area". Turn south on Park County Road 96. Drive for 0.9 - 1.0 mile and bear right (west) at a marked intersection. After 0.4 miles, reach the entrance station (pay an entrance fee). Continue south on Road 96 for campgrounds and climbing areas along both sides of the road.

SETTING UP
CAMP

Camp at one of several USFS campgrounds along the road through the canyon (Blue Mountain, Cove, Riverside, Spillway, Springer Gulch). Spillway Campground, close to the crags and bouldering, provides pit toilets, picnic tables, water, garbage cans and fire grates for $10.00 per night. The campgrounds fill up on busy summer weekends so try to reserve a site in advance. The campgrounds are open May 1 through October 5.
For reservations 1-877-444-6777 or www.recreation.gov
For more information about campgrounds:
www.forestcamping.com/dow/rockymtn/pikecmp.htm

Spacious campsites with flat spots for tent or car abound in Elevenmile Canyon

HOTELS &
MOTELS

We had a hard time finding Lake George, much less motels in Lake George. The first time, I drove right through "town" without noticing it. When I stopped at the gas station, they told me I'd passed town a mile back. However, the camping is terrific with gorgeous scenery, spacious flat sites and close to the river and climbing.

SHOPPING &
GROCERIES

**Starky's General Store**
38316 US 24, Lake George, (719) 748-3884
Starky's General Store sells beer, wine, groceries, and fishing tackle.

**Ponderosa Country Store**
39608 US 24, (719) 748-3430
Drive about one mile east past the junction of US 24 and on Park County Road 96 to the Ponderosa Country Store, which sells the only gasoline in town. They sell some food and other necessities.

**Sinclair (for Propane)**
2839 US Highway 24, Florissant
(719) 748-8080

RESTAURANTS
& COFFEE

**Mountain Shadows Inn**, 38321 US 24, Lake George, (719) 748-3833
Mountain Shadows Inn serves sandwiches for lunch and Mexican food, steaks or seafood for dinner. They lack a no-smoking section and when we were there, enough patrons smoked that we decided to order our cinnamon roll to go. The cinnamon buns are very big and gooey and the kids liked them.

Choose among several restaurants in Lake George or drive to nearby Florissant.

## What Else Can We Do That's Fun? (page 115)

# ELEVENMILE CANYON

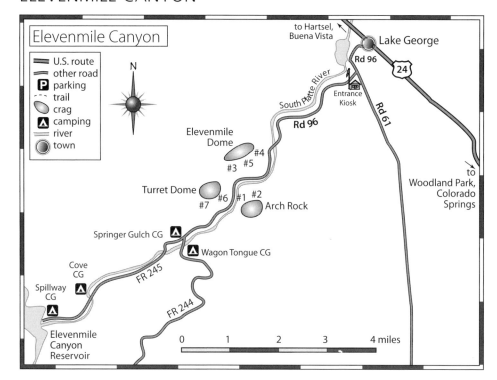

## Arch Rock

Drive 4.0 miles from the junction to Arch Rock, which is on the left and park at either of two pull-outs along the road. The first is on the right (west) side and the second on the left side (east) or park at the nearby Elevenmile Picnic Area. A short, steep climber's trail leads up to the crag. Be sure to include nuts, stoppers, and cams in your gear set.

A little one enjoys a bit of fishing in the South Platte River

### ___1. Hollow Flake 5.6 ★★★

GPS: 8,178 ft        13S 0464828 UTM 4310037

*Hollow Flake,* a crack and face climb, provides a good introduction to crack climbing. Start climbing near a pine tree about 30-40 ft left of a large left-facing corner. Climb up the left side of a flake left of the corner. Use long slings here to avoid rope drag and protect the second. Traverse about 15 ft right along the top of the flake into the corner. Continue up the corner to the top.

The rope will run best if the second climbs up to the top and all climbers rappel with one rope from two bolts with D-rings. However, for climbers who do not know how to rappel, it is possible to set up the climb as a toprope using long slings at the top and a directional near the top of the corner.

Another option would be to belay atop the spacious ledge and teach the other climbers how to rappel from here.

From this anchor, it's possible to also toprope the 5.10 climb on the face and arête just right of the corner.

### ___2. The Staircase 5.5 ★

GPS: 8,318 ft        13S 0464826 UTM 4310056

*The Staircase* will give new climbers a great taste of multi-pitch climbing in a gorgeous setting. From the top, they can enjoy views of the river.

Walk about 150 feet left of *Hollow Flake* to the base of a long, right-facing corner. Stem and jam up the large corner to a good ledge (place an anchor here). Another pitch of stemming reaches the top. Near the top of the pitch, either go straight up the direct finish, a 5.8 offwidth, or step left and go around this section. If going around, make sure to place gear with long runners along the traverse left.

When we climbed this, the leader went straight up without gear, in order to avoid rope drag.

When belaying at the top of the crack, the rope swings back deep into the offwidth and I couldn't flip it out. The hand jams are fairly deep in the crack, and a small kid would most likely have difficulties reaching the jams (provided that they know how to jam!).

It may be better to belay on the ledge left of the offwidth, bring the second up to this ledge, and then lead a short third pitch around to the left to reach the top.

**Descent:** Walk right (south) along the top of the cliff and follow a faint climber's trail down along the right side. The descent is safe — not exposed and in the trees but long enough to make comfortable shoes for the downclimb desirable.

Sibylle Hechte on Hollow Flake 5.6     Photograph by Tristan Hechtel

## Elevenmile Dome

Drive 2.8 miles from the junction to Elevenmile Dome, which is on the right (west) side of the road. Park at a pulloff near the south end of the dome. A faint trail heads in toward the cliff and parallels the cliff base. Be sure to pack nuts, stoppers, cams and **two ropes**.

### ___3. Moby Grape 5.7 ★★★
GPS: 13S 0464 UTM 4310

*Moby Grape* is fun, fairly low-angle and not very strenuous. Some people say that *Moby Grape* is easier than *Hollow Flake*, a 5.6 on Arch Rock. And it's hard to beat the approach!

From the pullout, walk back north along the road until below a large right-facing corner. Hike about 200 ft uphill through some talus to the base of the corner.

Climb up the prominent corner, using nuts and small cams for the crack. Belay at a two-bolt anchor with rappel rings just right of the crack. From here, rappel or toprope with two ropes. Caution! A 60-meter rope does not reach the ground from the anchor; make sure to bring a second rope.

### ___4. Original Sin  5.9+

Directly right of *Moby Grape* a line of bolts protects the face of *Original Sin*. This can be toproped (using two ropes) after leading *Moby Grape*. The stance at the top of *Moby Grape* is sloping and doesn't provide very good footholds, thus the belay is uncomfortable. *Original Sin* is not steep and a good introduction to thin granite friction climbing. It follows small edges and fingertip nubbins to the anchors. About 9 bolts exist on the route, but they're difficult to see until you reach them.

Elevenmile Dome

### ____5. Happy Trails 5.6 ★★

From the base of *Moby Grape*, walk back down to the road and walk north about 200 ft. Walk and scramble up a ramp to a ledge with a large prominent tree, the start of *Happy Trails*. Face climb up slabby friction to a two-bolt anchor with rappel rings. The first bolt is about 30 ft above the ledge; this may be too runout for the beginning 5.6 leader. Green's book states that this climb has six bolts; we found only three bolts but this seemed an adequate amount for the difficulty of the climbing. Place small TCUs a bit higher up on the route, but nothing before the first bolt. Rappel to the ledge and toprope from the ledge with one 60-meter rope.

*Happy Trails* may be scary for the beginning leader but it's a great route on which to take people. The climbing is very straightforward (no chimneys, stemming or jamming) and not at all strenuous. The ledge by the tree is quite wide and the ramp not very steep, but inexperienced climbers may feel more comfortable if they are anchored to the tree.

Happy Trails

# Turret Dome

Drive 4.0 miles from the junction and park at the Elevenmile Picnic Area. Cross the footbridge and turn left to hike west for five to ten minutes beside the river. Pass the picnic tables on the right and then the trail winds along close to the river. Access to the closest climb, *Sunshine Slab*, is fairly flat and takes about five minutes. The next few climbs lie further uphill along the dome's south side. Again, your rack should include nuts, stoppers, cams and **two ropes**.

### ____6. Sunshine Slab 5.0 – 5.4 ★★

**P1.** One can choose among many possibilities on the way up the low-angle slab. The right side offers more cracks to place protection. The left side, to a small tree, offers fewer gear placements but the climbing is easy. From the tree, rappel off fixed slings with rappel rings (two ropes). Beware of nasty stinging ants at this tree!

**P2.** If continuing up to the top of the slab, the climb joins *Jaws* and finishes on the 5.4 third pitch—a right leaning crack. Green refers to this as a hand crack, but his hands must be much larger than mine! Luckily one can climb face holds to the right of the crack and on the crack's sides much of the way up. After a tricky first move to get into the crack, the angle and difficulties both lessen. At the end of the crack, traverse right for a while to reach an easy way up through the summit overhangs.

**Descent:** Continue north along the dome's top and downclimb cracks and corners toward the saddle. From the saddle, a faint climbers trail heads downhill to the picnic area.

150-foot rappel

I thought that the descent was as difficult as the slabs below. It's exposed and I would suggest belaying (or short-roping) beginners on the descent. For novices, it might be better to rappel off the ant tree (or a different tree) after one pitch.

### ___7. Guide's Route 5.6 ★

For those who want a longer and slightly harder climb, *Guide's Route* provides another option. Walk another five to ten minutes uphill past the start of *Sunshine Slab*. Continue uphill past the large arch to a right-facing corner with parallel cracks.

**P1.** Climb the left 5.6 crack up about 40 ft, step right to the right-hand crack and follow this to a stance between this crack and the next.

**P2.** Follow discontinuous cracks to a belay beneath the summit overhangs.

**P3.** Surmount the summit overhangs by wandering from ledge to ledge along the easiest route to reach the top. Or, if the weather threatens, traverse left on the slabs toward the saddle.

# THE SOUTH PLATTE

Scenic pine forests, rivers with excellent fishing or swimming, and access points to the famed Colorado Trail are near the climbing areas. Also, enjoy the beautiful, remote, free camping near the climbs.

Approaches to the climbs vary in length. Some are short, such as the approach to Bucksnort Slab or Sphinx Rock. Both of these cliffs have excellent beginner and moderate routes. I will describe routes on Bucksnort Slab, Sphinx Rock, and the Turkey Rock area. Bucksnort Slab has a very short approach—less than five minutes. Sphinx Rock has a slightly longer approach with an easy friction route that makes it well worth the hike up to the cliff.

Sallie Greenwood climbing *Lickety Split* 5.7

## The Thumbs Up and Thumbs Down on the South Platte Area.....

 **Pros:** Short approaches; beautiful scenery; great camping with gorgeous fall colors; quality friction and crack climbing on good rock; easy climbs; river.

 **Cons:** Rough dirt road to Turkey Rock; remote; few amenities.

## Climbing here is mostly...

## Logistics at a Glance

**Approach**
1 minute flat to 20 minutes uphill, depending on the crag.

**Food?**
Slim pickin's around Pine and Deckers.

**Rock Type**
Granite

**Cell Coverage**
No

**Climb Type**
2 ropes, nuts, stoppers, cams, kneepads for chimney. Some bolted faces.

**Hot Spots**
No

**Ages**
Any age
Some short approaches for older or disabled climbers.

**Dogs?**
Yes

**Camping?**
Some free primitive camping or U.S.F.S. sites for $12.00.

**Seasons**
Spring, Summer or Fall

## How many routes are here?*

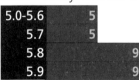

| 5.0-5.6 | 5 |
| 5.7 | 5 |
| 5.8 | 9 |
| 5.9 | 9 |

* This statistic is for reference only, not all climbs of these grades have been chosen for this book.

Take Highway 285 to Pine Junction and head south for 6.0 miles on Highway 126 to the small town of Pine, a National Historic District. Turn here left to reach Bucksnort Slab or Sphinx Rock. Continue straight for Turkey Rocks.

About 7.1 miles past Pine turn right on FS 550 at a sign for Wellington Lake and Buffalo Creek Recreation area. When driving down the dirt road, pass the Little Scraggy Trailhead for the Colorado Trail. After about one half mile, look for roadside pullouts to park for free camping. These primitive sites lack water, toilets, and any facilities. On the plus side, the camping here is peaceful, among beautiful ponderosa pines.

A few miles farther south on Highway 126, about 10 – 11 miles south of Pine, reach a U.S.F.S. campground, Kelsey Campground. Stay here amidst big pine trees in large well-spaced sites with picnic tables, fire grates, vault toilets and trash removal. The 17 sites have a 14-day limit and cost $12.00 per night. When we visited one Saturday in August; it was empty except for one site.

Johnny Molloy, author of *The Best in Tent Camping Colorado: A Guide for Car Campers who Hate RVs, Concrete Slabs, and Loud Portable Stereos,* recommends Buffalo Campground near Bailey.

Kelsey Campground

113

The Trip Guide

HOTELS &
MOTELS

### Meadow Creek Bed and Breakfast
13438 US Highway 285, Pine
(303) 838-4167    www.meadowcreekbb.com
Open year round: 8 a.m. – 7 p.m.
Go past Conifer, before Pine Junction, and off the frontage road. To treat
the family, check out this lovely B&B voted one of the Top 50 Inns in
America. They have extra rollaway beds for the kids and serve a full breakfast including eggs, bacon, casseroles, potatoes, and fruit.

SHOPPING &
GROCERIES

Few stores exist in the South Platte area, so bring everything necessary.
There are small stores in Deckers, including the **Deckers Coffee Shop**,
**Platte Valley Liquors**, and the **Deckers Store** which mainly sells beer
and soda pop.

### Pine Emporium
16714 Hwy. 126    www.nancycollectibles.com/tom-clark-gnomes.com
The Pine Emporium, at the junction to Sphinx Rock, sells ceramic gnomes
and has an incredible collection of unique gnomes by the artist Tom Clark.
The owner began collecting these gnomes in 1960 and showed us one that
the artist created in her likeness. For a unique present to take home to the
grandparents (if they're not already here) this shop can provide it!

RESTAURANTS
& COFFEE

### Elk Creek Restaurant
Elk Creek Restaurant is a short distance south of Pine, toward Deckers.
The owners of the Pine Emporium spoke of it favorably, but I haven't
eaten there myself. It's the only restaurant nearby, so give it a try.

### Bucksnort Saloon
15921 S. Elk Creek Road, Pine, (303) 838-0284
Continue north past Bucksnort Slab to the Bucksnort Saloon, a nice place
to stop for a beer and some bar food after a hot day's climbing.

OTHER
CLIMBING
GUIDES

*South Platte Rock*, Ken Trout, 1997.
*Serious Play*, Steve Dieckhoff, 2002.
*Rock Climbing Colorado*, Stewart Green, 1995.
*Front Range Topropes*, Fred Knapp, 2000.

EMERGENCY
INFO
&
MORE

### Hospitals
### Swedish Medical Center
501 E. Hampden Ave.
Englewood, CO
(303) 788-5000

# What Else Can We Do That's Fun?

## Bouldering

In his guidebook, *Colorado Bouldering* (revised 2006) Benningfield describes the excellent bouldering near Sheep's Nose, a cliff on the road into Turkey Rocks. Spread around dozens of granite boulders at 8,000 feet altitude, this will tire kids if the climbing hasn't done so! To find The Sheep's Nose boulders refer to the Turkey Rocks directions (see following pages) to Stump Road (Douglas County 68). Turn right and drive 1.8 miles to a dirt pull-out on the left side of the road. Cross the road and walk past a fence looking for a trail on the right. After about 175 yards up the trail, you'll encounter a boulderfield. Explore.

Onward

## Hiking

Keilty describes only one hike in this area, the Crags Trail off CO 24 near Divide. The approaches to Sphinx Rock or Turkey Rocks offer as much scenic beauty, bizarre rock formations, boulders to scramble on and caves to explore to satisfy any hiking urges.

If you want to inform yourself about more local hiking options, Jacobs' book describes the Colorado Trail, which has access right along FS 550.

**Sibylle's Travels**
**Great Reference**

*Best Hikes With Children in Colorado* by Maureen Keilty

*The Colorado Trail: The Official Guidebook* by Randy Jacobs

*Mountain Bike America: Colorado: An Atlas of Colorado's Greatest Off-Road Bicycle Rides* by Stephen Hlawaty.

Matt Flach on *Ragger Bagger* 5.8

115

MOUNTAIN
BIKING

### Mountain Biking

Hlawaty calls the Buffalo Creek Area, further along the dirt road described earlier for camping near Sphinx Rock, a mini mountain biking mecca. He mentions two trails in his book that start near here, the Baldy and Gashouse Gulch Trails. The trail starts on FS 550 past the primitive camping. The trail description is sufficiently detailed that rather than try to recap it here and risk omitting important details, I think it's best to buy or borrow his book, which also includes a map of the route.

### Horseback Riding

The M Lazy C Ranch, a dude ranch in nearby Lake George, offers hayrides, pack trips, carriage rides, and cattle drives.
(800) 289-4868    www.mlazyc.com

REST DAY
ACTIVITIES

### Boating, Water and Fishing
**Elevenmile State Park**
Fish, sail, windsurf and play in the water!
4229 CO Rd. 92, Lake George, CO 80827
(719) 748-3401    eleven.mile.park@state.co.us

**11-Mile Marina**
North shore of Elevenmile State Park
(719) 748-0317    www.11milemarina.com
The Marina rents boats, including powerboats, canoes, kayaks and paddleboats. They also provide outfitting and guide services.

**South Platte River Fishing**
Catch rainbow, brown and cutthroat trout, kokanee salmon, northern pike, small-mouth bass and carp.

### Museums and Wildlife
**Florissant Fossil Beds National Monument**
(719) 748-3253    www.nps.gov/flfo.com
Take the kids on hikes to see wildlife in the monument, including bighorn sheep, elk, antelope, cougars, and bears. If the animals are shy and won't stand still, head down two interpretive trails and then to the visitor center for fossil displays. The Florissant Fossil Beds are especially prolific repositories of butterfly and beetle fossils.

See the book below for great pictures:
*Florissant Butterflies: A Guide to the Fossil and Present Day Species of Central Colorado,* Thomas Emmel, Marc Mino, and Boyce Drummond, 1992.

**Colorado Wolf and Wildlife Center**
The center is about six miles west of Divide near Mile Marker 272 on the north side of the highway.    www.wolfeducation.org

---

**Sibylle's Travels**
Fishing
A local fisherman described this section of the South Platte River as one of the hardest, most challenging rivers anywhere to fish, however he has reaped a 12" – 14" brown and rainbow trout near the Elevenmile Picnic Area and a 6" – 18" trout between the Elevenmile Reservoir and Spinney Reservoir.

# THE SOUTH PLATTE

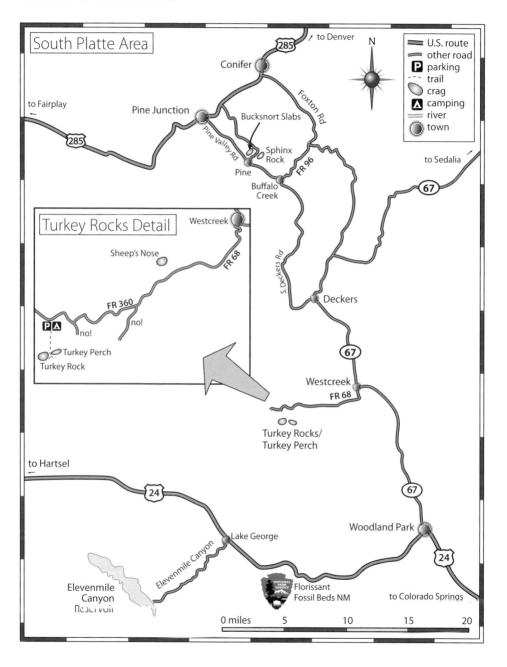

South Platte Area

to Denver
285
N

| | U.S. route |
| | other road |
| P | parking |
| | trail |
| | crag |
| A | camping |
| | river |
| | town |

Conifer

Foxton Rd

to Fairplay

Pine Junction

Bucksnort Slabs

285

Pine Valley Rd

Sphinx Rock

FR 96

Pine

to Sedalia

67

Buffalo Creek

Westcreek

Turkey Rocks Detail

Sheep's Nose

S. Deckers Rd

FR 68

FR 360

no!

no!

P A no!

Turkey Perch
Turkey Rock

Deckers

67

Westcreek

FR 68

Turkey Rocks/
Turkey Perch

to Hartsel

24

67

67

24

Woodland Park

Lake George

Elevenmile Canyon

Florissant
Fossil Beds NM

to Colorado Springs

Elevenmile
Canyon
Reservoir

| 0 miles | 5 | 10 | 15 | 20 |

## SPHINX ROCK

     River crossing.

To reach Sphinx Rock and Bucksnort Slab, turn left (north, across the street from the North Fork Volunteer Fire Department) on 4th Street which turns into Elk Creek Road. Drive up the winding canyon about 0.4 – 0.5 miles to Sphinx Rock.

Park at a small pullout on the left near the cliff. Hike down toward the creek, cross on rocks or a plank across the creek and head up to the cliff. In fall, we encountered water about ankle deep, but in spring the river is probably too deep to easily cross. The road that leads to the house across the river is private property and was posted as such when I last climbed there. Ask private landowners for permission to cross their land to access climbing but please don't trespass. Also check local climbing shops, land management agencies, etc. for current conditions, which may change.

### ___1. Lickety Split  5.7 R ★

The other guidebooks both describe two climbs here, *Plinth*, 5.7 - 5.8 R, on the left, and *Lickety Split* to the right of it. When we climbed here in August 2005, only one of these routes, *Lickety Split*, still had bolts.

**P1.** Lead up an easy friction slab for about 30 feet to the first bolt, an old 1/4" buttonhead. Continue to the second bolt, another 1/4" relic (the climbing remains easy to this point). For bolts three and four, where the moves become thinner, shiny new fat bolts protect the moves.

**P2.** Stop and belay on the slab at a two-bolt anchor (no rap rings) or continue on past three more bolts to the top. Bring cams for the top, from small TCUs to a #1 Camalot (since we found no fixed bolted anchor, but a very good crack).

For more climbing, toprope *Plinth* sans bolts.

**Descent:** At the top, turn left (west) and hike down a faint climber's trail to the base (about ten minutes).

Tristan Hechtel on *Classic Dihedral* 5.7+

## BUCKSNORT SLAB

Possible stuck rope on rappel; crowded on weekends

To reach Bucksnort Slab from Pine Junction, turn left (north) on Elk Creek Road, which turns to dirt and drive about one mile to a slab above the road on the left. Park at a pullout past Bucksnort Slab and walk back down the road to a narrow climber's trail heading up and right between boulders and head to the base of the obvious dihedral. The base area is flat and spacious and the approach trail is only steep for short sections. For a more pleasant outing bring two 50m ropes, stoppers, nuts and cams.

### ___2. Classic Dihedral 5.7+ ★★★

Jam and layback a hand and finger crack occasionally using some face holds on the side. On the wide section, a #3 Camalot protects the moves. At the top, where the crack widens again, layback past this section and then step left to a belay stance with many bolts. There are enough bolts that one party can rappel off one set and another tie in to a second set. Use two ropes to rappel, and pull the ropes carefully so that they don't get stuck in the crack.

Climbers who forget the second rope can continue on to the top on a short second pitch and walk off the back.

160-foot rappel

# TURKEY PERCH AND TURKEY ROCK

Some of the best crack climbing in Colorado is at the Turkey Rock area. Practice on Yosemite-style splitter hand cracks with good quality rock, reasonable approaches, and good weather.

From Pine Junction, drive south to Deckers, then 8.7 miles past Deckers to Westcreek (about a half mile past the turn-off) and continue on County Road 68. Turn west on Stump Road (Road 68) for 2.5 miles to Forest Road 360. Drive a rutted dirt road for 1.7 miles to Big Turkey Campground (closed). Most parties continue on rougher terrain another 0.8 miles to the Turkey Rock pull-out (unmarked). It's possible to camp anywhere in the forest at unimproved sites with no amenities, but it's peaceful and free.

From the turnaround, look for a trail that heads to the saddle. Hike up the switchbacks for 10 to 15 minutes to reach a saddle between Turkey Rock on the right and Turkey Perch on the left. Turn left and head slightly downhill and across to the base of Turkey Perch, a cliff broken by numerous cracks ranging from finger size to chimneys. *Reefer Madness* is on the left end of the crag and the next two climbs are near the right side.

Turkey Perch

121

### ___3. Reefer Madness 5.8 ★★

Start left of a metal memorial plaque and stem
and jam up two cracks. Move into the left-
leaning hand and finger crack and climb up to
a horizontal break. Traverse left below the lip,
using large stoppers or a #2 Camalot to protect
the traverse for the second. Belay at the top of
the crack (gear) or at the large tree. *Reefer Madness* requires good jamming technique and/or
tape! Descend by walking off the back.

### ___4. Ragger Bagger 5.8+

The crack just to the right of *Reefer Madness*
is another 5.8 hand and fist crack. The bulge
at the top may prove a little tricky with some
chimney and stemming moves to surmount the
final bulge but the bottom and middle of this
crack are very pleasant with good, solid
hand jams.

> **The two cracks below lie on a buttress
> near the right end of the rock, separat-
> ed by chimneys on either side and with
> a large block at the top.**

### ___5. Honky Jam Ass Crack 5.7 ★

Both this crack and its neighbor are on the large
side—up to 3 inches. Though rated easier than
*Reefer Madness*, I think the rating is for those with
large hands. Still, it's a great route to practice
jamming technique. Hike to the top to toprope
either this or *Left Handed Jew*.

### ___6. Left Handed Jew 5.7 ★

After climbing *Honky Jam Ass Crack*, try this one
as well to perfect jamming technique. Bring
enough larger cams if uncomfortable leading
cracks of this size to protect them adequately.
*Left Handed Jew*, much like the crack beside it,
relies mostly on jamming technique with a few
face moves on the traverse near the top. Getting
out of the crack at the top proves a bit tricky.
Descend by walking off the back.

Sarah Watso1 on **Times Square** 5.8          Photograph by Dan McDonnell

# SHELF ROAD

Climbers from Colorado's Front Range migrate to Shelf Road's dry sunny cliffs, especially during winter months when the high desert environment provides an escape from the chill. Weekends see crowds at the more popular crags, especially the recently developed Cactus Cliff. Weekday climbing, however, can often bring solitude. I've climbed here mid-week November through January, with daytime highs in the 60s and 70s, and seen no one else.

The area is known for its well-bolted limestone with vertical routes spanning the 5.9 – 5.12 range (a few easier routes check in as low as 5.5). Most of the climbs feature crimpy edges or sporadic pockets with occasional bulges on near-vertical rock. The Shelf Road area is comprised of nearly a dozen major crags, together housing a thousand routes. Cactus Cliff has become the most popular destination and boasts over 150 routes on its south-facing and often wind-sheltered walls. Even on a cool day in the 40s, routes in the direct sun feel sweltering hot. Older kids who climb up to 5.9 will find a variety of routes to climb and a few to lead. Occasionally you'll see the Boulder (Colorado) Rock Club's junior climbing team training here en masse, but usually it's the stray parent who brings a kid or two.

Shelf Road tends to mainly attract locals on weekends, perhaps because it's mostly a cooler season climbing area. Most vacationing families travel in summer, when temperatures at Shelf Road can hit 100° F or more. Serious climbers—without mortgages, kids, or full-time jobs—who travel in winter, often eschew Shelf Road for its lack of hard routes in the 5.13 to 5.14 range. If you have a week off in fall or spring, Shelf Road offers a plethora of fine routes.

I will describe easy routes on Cactus Cliff and Spiney Ridge as well as the Contest Wall and Freeform Wall in Sand Gulch. The Contest Wall gets afternoon shade offering a nice alternative on hot days. Other popular crags include The Bank, The Gallery and The Dark Side (a decent summer area). Anyone planning on an extended stay, however, should pick up the guide, *Shelf Road Rock* by Knapp, Thompson & Aschert, and explore the many options not covered here. Since most routes are sport climbs with modern lowering anchors, the area is ripe for family adventure.

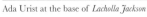
Ada Urist at the base of *Lacholla Jackson*

## The Thumbs Up and Thumbs Down on Shelf Road ........................

 **Pros:** Most routes provide a flat base area (Cactus Cliff and Spiney Ridge); several easy routes are well suited for kids or beginners. It's a short drive to Cañon City, a major tourist center with many amenities and fun family activities. Cactus Cliff is hospitably warm in the winter.

 **Cons:** Longish but mellow hike to Cactus Cliff due to a new parking lot. Some loose rock. You may want to bring helmets, at least for the kids, and leave the youngest children away from the base of the climb. Wasps, cactus spines, rattlesnakes. The south-facing cliffs are toasty in the summer.

## Climbing here is mostly...

## Logistics at a Glance ........................

**Approach**
1 mile easy hike to Cactus Cliff or 20 min steeper hike to Contest Wall.

**Food?**
Cañon City nearby, refer to text for details.

**Rock Type**
Limestone

**Cell Coverage**
Yes, from Sand Gulch campground and from parking lot at trailhead.

**Climb Type**
Bolted sport climbs. Rope and quickdraws.

**Hot Spots**
Free wireless at the Cañon City library.

**Ages**
Best for ages 6 and up. The limiting factor at Cactus Cliff is the length of the easy hike (about 1 mile).

**Dogs?**
Dogs allowed in campground and at cliffs. Please use a leash.

**Camping?**
BLM sites, $4.00 a night or Cañon City has commercial sites. See text for more details.

**Seasons**
Fall, Winter, Spring, Summer can be too warm.

## How many routes are here?*

| Cactus Cliff | | Spiney Ridge | | Sand Gulch | |
|---|---|---|---|---|---|
| 5.0-5.6 | 1 | 5.0-5.6 | | 5.0-5.6 | |
| 5.7 | 3 | 5.7 | | 5.7 | |
| 5.8 | 4 | 5.8 | 4 | 5.8 | 2 |
| 5.9 | 18 | 5.9 | 4 | 5.9 | 5 |

\* This statistic is for reference only, not all climbs of these grades have been chosen for this book.

GETTING
THERE

**Directions from Cañon City:** Shelf Road is a little over an hour drive from Colorado Springs. Take highway 50 to Cañon City, then turn north on Field Avenue, which lies between Raynolds and Orchard Avenues (these both have traffic lights).

Field Avenue changes into County Road 9 and then turns into Shelf Road. Continue north on Shelf Road for 11.6 miles until the pavement ends. Follow the dirt road for another 1.1 miles, for a total of 12.7 miles, and turn left into Sand Gulch campground.

Sand Gulch campground GPS: 13 S 0479999 UTM 4274326
Elevation: 6,150'

SETTING UP
CAMP

### Sibylle's Travels
#### Camping at Shelf

Behind some of the Sand Gulch campsites, my son found fossilized brachiopods (like seashells). They're small, but fairly abundant and kids like collecting them.

The BLM provides campgrounds at Sand Gulch and The Bank. These fill up on weekends, so find a site early. None supply water, so bring a good supply, especially during hot weather. The campgrounds provide picnic tables, fire rings and tent platforms. At the time of writing, the BLM charged $4.00 per night at self-pay stations; you'll need exact change or a checkbook. Pit toilets are available at the Sand Gulch and Bank campgrounds, but on busy weekends they run out of toilet paper. There is a toilet near the former parking area for Cactus Cliff. The BLM does not provide garbage cans; bring empty garbage bags to haul out your trash.

### Camping Hazards
Cactus spines, rattlesnakes, wasps, and mosquitoes.

In addition to campgrounds near the cliffs, you can try any of more than 10 commercial campgrounds near Cañon City. Most of these offer RV hookups and some provide added attractions, like go-carts, a giant slide, mini-golf, hiking, swimming, fishing, cabins, a pool, and a shuttle. http://www.canoncity.com/canon/visitors/camping.html

HOTELS &
MOTELS

Since Cañon City lies close to a major tourist attraction (Royal Gorge) you'll find abundant dining and accommodation choices, as well as many fun family-oriented activities. For complete lodging information head to www.canoncity.com/canon/visitors/lodging.html.

**The Orchard Bed & Breakfast**, 1824 Pinion Avenue, Brookside
2 miles from Cañon City.
(719) 275-0072, (877) 212-0497, www.theorchardbandb.com

### Pet and kid friendly options:

**The Best Western**, 1925 Fremont Drive, Cañon City
(719) 275-3377, Reservations: 800-231-7317, www.bestwestern.com
The Best Western lies off of Highway 50 offers great deals during the off-season. The rooms are large, some with two queen beds and a sleeper couch, a microwave, a refrigerator, and—best of all, they welcome your best friend – the family dog!

**Quality Inn And Suites**, Hwy. 50 & Dozier Ave., Cañon City
(719) 275-8676

### Grocery Stores
**Safeway** at 15th and Highway 50 (Royal Gorge Boulevard)
1414 Main St., Cañon City, (719) 275-5221

**City Market** just off of Highway 50. 1703 Fremont Dr. (719) 275-1595

### Propane
**Cañon Rental**, 401 S. 9th, (719) 275-0615

**HoochieMamma Mountaineering**, 1218 Royal Gorge Blvd.
Cañon City, CO 81212, (719) 275-22931
Stop in this friendly shop for whatever climbing equipment you may need,
included the complete guide to Shelf Road if you plan an extended stay here.

**Higher Limits**, 224 Main St.
Cañon City, CO 81212, (719) 276-0766

**Alfonso's Mexican Food**, 2801 E. Main St., (719) 276-0186
Along Highway 50 you'll find the ubiquitous Wendy's and a Taco Bell, as
well as many good local establishments. Our favorite take-out is Alfonso's
Supertaco/Mexican Food which makes huge burritos. I like the fish burrito
and my then 11-year old son liked the vegetarian variety. One day at the
cliff, while trying to talk me into driving to Alfonso's he asked,"Mom, if
I lead that whole climb without any falls will you take me to Alfonso's?"
"Sure," I replied, thinking there was no chance of that. Tristan proceeded
to lead, on-sight, with no falls, his first 5.11b.

**Hastings Coffee Shop** also Books, Music & Video
1811 Fremont Dr., Cañon City, (719) 276-1500
Opens at 6:30 am

**McClellan Grill & Brewin Company**
413 Main Street, Cañon City, (719) 276-3400

**Main Street Express (Deli and Coffeehouse)**
617 Main Street, Cañon City, (719) 276-0747

**Pizza Madness**
509 Main Street, Cañon City, (719) 276-3088

**Big Daddy's Diner**
420 Royal Gorge Blvd., Cañon City, (719) 276-8468

# What Else Can We Do That's Fun?

REST DAY
ACTIVITIES

### Rafting

50905 W. Hwy. 50, (800) 530-8212, www.waorafting.com

Several raft companies offer day trips on the Arkansas River. One of my favorites: Whitewater Adventure Outfitters

### Royal Gorge Railroad

401 Water St., (888) 724-5748, www.royalgorgeroute.com

In summer, trains depart from the historic Santa Fe Depot several times daily on a 24-mile round trip that takes about 2 hours. In fall and winter, trains run on weekends only. Both open-air observation cars and closed coaches run along the river, 1000 ft below the rim of the granite cliffs that tower above the gorge.

### Royal Gorge Bridge & Park     www.royalgorgebridge.com

The world's highest suspension bridge, the Royal Gorge Bridge, spans the gorge 1,053 ft above the Arkansas River. The Royal Gorge Bridge and Park offers rides on an aerial tram, a steep incline railway to the canyon floor, an antique replica carousel, and a petting zoo with burro rides. Drive north from town along Highway 50 and you can't miss the signs for the bridge.

MUSEUMS

### Dinosaur Depot Museum

330 Royal Gorge Blvd, (719) 269-7150, www.dinosaurdepot.com

The Dinosaur Depot, a museum in Cañon City, shows the world's most complete Stegosaurus, just one example of the many fossils found at the Garden Park Fossil area on the road from Cañon City to Shelf Road. At the Cleveland Quarry, roadside signs and a picnic area mark the sites where scientists found dinosaur bones from several species. Just 0.1 mile north of here, at the Marsh Quarry, scientists found the first specimen of Diplodocus, Stegosaurus, Tyrannosaurus, and Brontosaurus. Paleontologists also found fossils of Allosaurus, Apatosaurus, and others. You can hike a 1/4-mile nature trail complete with exhibits that describe the native plants, animals and fossils. Open late May through early September.

### Gold Mine Rock Shop

44864 Highway 50, (719) 276-9353

While driving north, you can stop at the Gold Mine Rock Shop about 8.0 miles west of Cañon City (my son wouldn't let me drive past). The shop sells souvenirs, crystals and agates. They have a big collection of fish fossils and onyx carvings.

REST DAY
ACTIVITIES

### Buckskin Joe Frontier Town

1193 Fremont County Road 3A, (719) 275-5149   www.buckskinjoes.com
A "real" old west town with hourly gun fights, live entertainment, barnyard
animals for the kids, and all you want in an "old west" town.

### City Park

This park lies on the corner of Hwy. 50 and 3rd Street. Here you'll find picnic
tables, toilets, and grass to run around on. It's close to the prison museum.

### Skyline Drive

This airy one lane, one-way road offers a bird's eye view of Cañon City.
From the west edge of town, drive 2.9 miles on Highway 50, passing
mile marker 278. Just past the Razor Ridge Trading Post, turn right on a
narrow road and go beneath an old stone arch. This road, built in 1903
by prisoners, rises 800 feet above the valley and gives a great view of the
surrounding mountains.

### Shelf Road    www.goldbeltbyway.com

The road itself is part of the Gold Belt Tour and a National Scenic Byway.
The website below discusses Byway history, wildlife along Shelf Road and
offers driving time for the scenic loop.

### Wolf Sanctuary   www.missionwolf.com

You can visit a remote wolf sanctuary in a day trip from Cañon City. See
the web site for details.

OTHER
CLIMBING
GUIDES

*Shelf Road Rock: A Complete Climbing Reference*, Fred Knapp, Rick Thompson
and Rich Aschert, 2005.

EMERGENCY
INFO
&
MORE

**St. Thomas More Hospital**
Off of 15th Street about one-half
mile north of Highway 50, can tend
to any ailments.
1019 Sheridan St.
(719) 275-3381.

**BLM**
3170 E. Main
(719) 269-8500

**Cañon City Chamber of Commerce**
403 Royal Gorge Blvd. (Highway 50)
(719) 275-2331    (800) 876-7922

**Cañon City Public Library**
516 Macon Ave.
(719) 269-9020
Wireless internet access

131

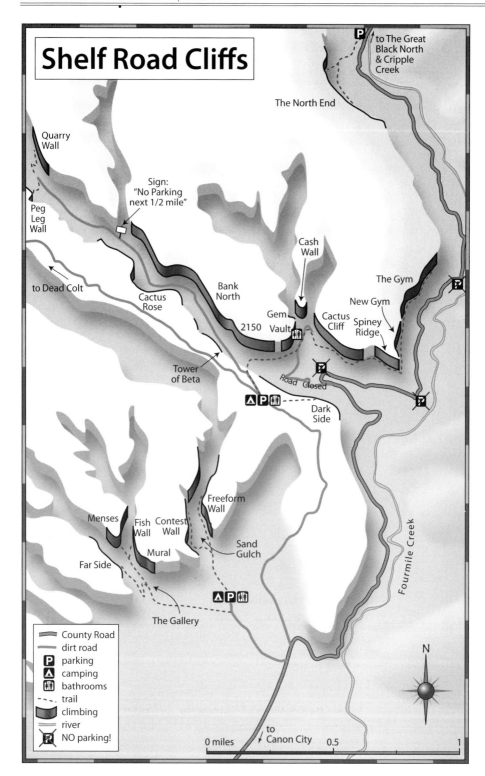

# Shelf Road Cliffs

Quarry Wall

Peg Leg Wall

The North End

to The Great Black North & Cripple Creek

Sign: "No Parking next 1/2 mile"

Cash Wall

to Dead Colt

Bank North

Cactus Rose

The Gym

New Gym

Gem Vault

2150

Cactus Cliff

Spiney Ridge

Tower of Beta

Road Closed

Dark Side

Freeform Wall

Menses

Fish Wall

Contest Wall

Sand Gulch

Far Side

Mural

The Gallery

Fourmile Creek

N

County Road
dirt road
P parking
⛺ camping
🚻 bathrooms
trail
climbing
river
NO parking!

to Canon City

0 miles          0.5          1

## CACTUS CLIFF

**Approach**: At one time, Cactus Cliff offered the shortest approach of any Shelf Road crag, thanks to an unmaintained access road that veered off the Shelf Road. However, due to liability concerns and landowner issues, the BLM opted to close the road in November of 2006. The Rocky Mountain Field Institute with help from AmeriCorps volunteers created a new trail from the newly expanded parking lot at The Bank to Cactus Cliff. The new trail is approximately 1.2 miles and may not be suitable for the smallest children.

After the trail reaches the former parking area, an unmarked but obvious path leads east along the base of Cactus Cliff. You'll see the cliff above and to the left of the trail. Cactus Cliff curves like a ship's prow, with the left (west) side facing slightly west so that it gets morning shade and afternoon sun. The right (eastern) flank faces more east and south, providing pleasant morning sunshine.

 Heed the NO PARKING signs along Shelf Road. Even if a pullout looks safe and adequate for your car; do not park. Tickets of $50-$75 are given out liberally.

Young climber at the base of Spiney Ridge

Far left side of Cactus Cliff

### ___1. Crynoid Corner 5.7 ★★★

You'll find *Crynoid Corner,* at the far left (west) end of Cactus Cliff. Just past the old parking lot, stone steps lead up and left. At a fork in the trail, turn left and continue for about three minutes to the climb.

This route follows a hand crack in a right-facing corner close to the left cliff edge. Though rated easier than *LaCholla Jackson,* some people find it more difficult because it requires crack climbing technique. One or two moves entail liebacking or jamming, which may stump someone who climbs primarily in the gym. 9 clips.

 **Not Recommended Climbs:** If referencing *Shelf Road Rock* in addition to this book, many other moderate routes are here for exploring. Several of them receive a thumbs down.

**The Hourglass 5.8**
As a new route, we found it to be dangerously loose and rotten. Time and traffic may improve this, but ask someone who's climbed it recently before venturing onto this one. Located on the right side (before broken choss) of the 1st wall encountered on the trail; it's about the 25th route on Cactus Cliff.

**Commitment 5.9**
I found this route very strenuous and think it's hard for the grade. If you're unsure of getting up over bulges, let some young rope gun have this lead.

**Bur-Har-Bur 5.9**
While the 5.9 rating might tempt an effort on this route, many other 5.9s offer much better quality rock. Loose rock along the climb and on the ledge could fall and injure people below. This climb is located 3 routes right of *Kodachrome.*

**Fully Equipped 5.9+**
Loose rock with guano-covered handholds creates a truly unpleasant climbing experience. Perhaps traffic will clean this one up over time. Located on the far right side of Cactus Cliff just before Spiney Ridge is encountered.

### ____2. Kalahari Sidewinder 5.8 ★

General consensus is that the route is hard for the grade, as it's a somewhat strenuous and slightly awkward crack. My son, who leads me up 5.11 face climbs, says it's hard for 5.8 and considers *Chompin' at the Cholla* (5.9) easier. If you like cracks, and your friends are good at jamming, this would be a good choice. If not, you're better off trying some 5.9 face climbs. 4 clips.

### ____3. Kodachrome 5.9

*Kodachrome* is a great line located about 20 ft to the right of *Kalahari Sidewinder*. Climbing the corner requires stemming, chimneying, and hand jams so crack fans may find this easier than pure sport climbers. If you choose to climb directly along the line of bolts, on the arête, the route difficulty increases to hard 5.10. The ledge at the top poses a danger in the event of excess slack during a fall. 4 clips.

Lats Wall
Cluster of routes

**____4. Alexi's Climb** 5.5 ★★

From the old parking lot, follow the trail east for about five minutes (about 250 yards) until reaching a S/SE-facing alcove ont the left. Eight stone steps lead to a relatively flat area in front of an easy bolted slab on the left and a harder slab to the right. *Alexi's Climb* follows the bolts along the left slab.

From the ledge at the top of *Alexi's Climb*, I taught my son how to rappel and how to feed the rope through the anchors. Tristan led the climb and then belayed me up to the ledge. While I watched closely, he fed the rope through the anchor rings and set up the rappel. Teaching kids to thread the anchor is much less scary for both parent and child if there's a nice, spacious ledge for both to stand on while learning to do this correctly. 6 clips.
GPS: 13 S 0480770 UTH 4275849

**____5. Ian's Climb** 5.7 ★

Just a few steps to the right of *Alexi's Climb*, *Ian's Climb* follows a small right-facing corner. At 5.7, it's a bit tougher than *Alexi's Climb*. If your child or friend wants to try leading this climb, suggest that they traverse left a few feet below the top of the route to the same

anchors as *Alexi's* rather than continuing to the anchors shared by *Ian's* and the climb to the right (*Red Eclipse*, a 5.10c slab climb with tiny edges). 6 clips.

**____6. Ol'Four-Seven** 5.9 ★

Three bolted routes to the right of *Ian's Climb*, *Ol'Four-Seven* follows four bolts up a slab just left of a flake. It tops out on a large, flat ledge with good toprope anchors. For toproping, provide a directional to avoid a swing into the corner. 4 clips.

### ____7. Oscar de la Cholla 5.9 ★★

Just right of a gully and broken area about 50 steps east of the previous route, stone steps lead up to a small flat area. *Oscar de la Cholla* is the second bolted climb right of the gully. Face climb about 15 feet to a crack. Follow this for another 15 feet to a pedestal from which two cracks continue to the top. Just below the anchor, a narrow ledge provides good footholds, but the anchor is placed quite high for shorter climbers. 7 clips.

The author on *Oscar de la Cholla*

___**8. LaCholla Jackson** 5.8 ★★★★

Continue east past *Oscar* for about 150 feet to a large open corner with four bolted climbs on the left wall. *LaCholla Jackson*, perhaps the best 5.8 at Shelf, follows the small lieback crack on the right wall, about 15-20 feet right of the large main corner. This well-bolted crack eventually peters to face climbing on pockets. 10 clips and chain anchors.

___**9. Chompin' at the Cholla** 5.9 ★★

Continue walking east along the cliff, almost to the end. At a fork in the trail, take the left fork heading about 60 feet up to the cliff. A pillar forms a left-facing corner. From the top of the pillar (reached by stemming or face climbing) head left and over the bulge, which may contain long reaches for small kids. 8 clips and chain anchors.

*LaCholla Jackson*

*Chompin' at the Cholla*

139

## SPINEY RIDGE

**Approach**: An 8-12 minute stroll past Cactus Cliff leads to Spiney Ridge, the next crag to the east. The Thompson Alcove, a SW-facing wall at the left edge of the cliff, offers afternoon sun.

____**10. Damn Right I've Got the Moves** 5.9 ★★

This route follows a crack just left of *Stone of Ignorance* and should prove equally challenging. The fun jamming will prove a challenging technique for the novice climber. (Two more bolted routes just left of this finish up the routes left of *Cheers*. At 5.10d and 5.11b, they're beyond the scope of this book!)

____**11. Stone of Ignorance** 5.9 ★

*Stone of Ignorance* follows discontinuous cracks and face about 15 feet left of *Cheers*. The guidebook suggests three grades: 5.9, 5.10 or 5.11, depending on whether you climbed right of the bolts, left of the bolts, or directly up the middle. 7 clips.

____**12. Cheers** 5.8 ★★

With spaced-out bolts and a corner crack, this makes a better toprope than a lead. 6 clips.

# SAND GULCH

Within walking distance of Sand Gulch campground you can access either of 2 walls in Sand Gulch. The Contest Wall, the cliff you can see from the campground, faces slightly southeast and gets good early morning sun. Across the gulch, the Freeform Wall gets morning shade and sun quite late in the afternoon.

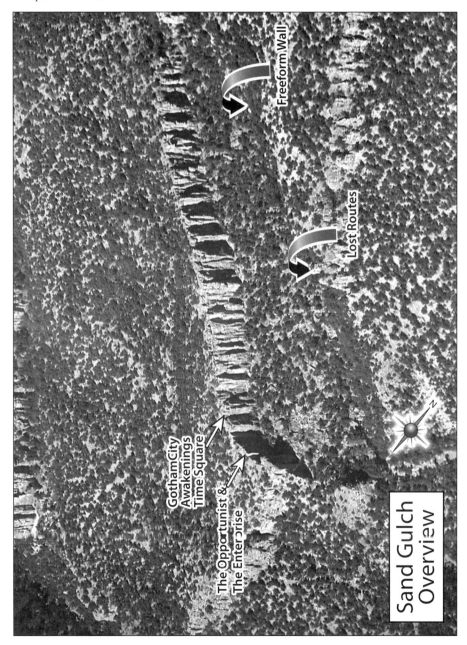

Freeform Wall

Lost Routes

GothamCity
Awakenings
Time Square

The Opportunist &
The Enterprise

Sand Gulch
Overview

## CONTEST WALL

**Approach**: The Contest Wall faces slightly southeast, receiving early morning sun. From the Sand Gulch campground a marked trail leads down to the streambed which is followed to the stairs leading to the Contest Wall. From the left edge of the wall, walk uphill (north) for about four minutes to a prominent corner with a large juniper tree overhanging the top of the wall.

### ___13. The Opportunist 5.9 ★★★
This meandering line up a featured wall may have been a trad route at one time. However, it's only seen traffic recently. 9 bolts.

### ___14. Enterprise 5.9+ ★★★★
An even better and longer version of its neighbor—an unending route that tackles one of the biggest expanses at Sand Gulch. 10 black coldshuts to a 2-bolt anchor.

### ___15. Gotham City 5.10a ★
Begin in the center of an alcove and head up a black slab to an upper wall on the left side of a dihedral. Beware, your rope may pull into a cactus.

### ___16. Awakenings 5.9+ ★★
Begin just right of the previous route and wander all around past hard to clip bolts until you get to the anchor.

### ___17. Times Square 5.8 ★★
This climb, not suited for the beginning 5.8 leader, follows ledges and corners left of the arête and right of a large crack. The first bolt is about 20 ft above the ground and is often stick-clipped. The route wanders away from the bolts and the anchor can be hard to reach from the ledge. However, once you've got the rope up, it's a fun route for everyone else to toprope! 7 clips.

*Times Square*

Contest Wall

# FREEFORM WALL

**Approach**: Head down the labeled trail to Sand Gulch from the north end of the day-use parking area. Follow signs directing you to veer uphill and right to the Freeform Wall. If you were at the previous routes on the Contest Wall, head back down the trail to the dry creek bed, turn up north (away from the day-use parking) and look for the Freeform Wall signs. *Barney*, your destination climb, is the obvious crack.

___**18. Barney** 5.9 ★★★

This fun and popular bolted crack doesn't actually require jamming. The last few moves may seem harder than its 5.9 rating. 7 clips.

___**19. Guilty by Association** 5.9

If you want to get more bang for your hike, head south to a short climb isolated by itself. This is also a pretty popular route. 2 clips.

Jonah Adelman on **Last 1/2 Inch** 5.7

# INDEPENDENCE PASS

Independence Pass offers incredibly varied climbing from short easy topropes with minimal approaches to multi-pitch sport routes to long easy trad climbs. The Pass comprises a number of cliffs and crags along the 38-mile road over Independence Pass from Twin Lakes on the east side of the divide to Aspen on the west side. It's a perfect summer spot with a nearby lake for swimming. When temperatures in Denver soar, Twin Lakes at 9,200 feet stays cool with daytime highs in the 70s.

Here in the heart of the Rockies, snow-capped peaks tower above roadside crags, snow-fed streams gurgle near the campsites, and marmots chase each other beside the road. Several fourteeners reside in the region including 14,433 foot-Mt. Elbert, Colorado's highest peak nestled beside one of the state's largest glacial lakes.

Some of the smaller crags, including Powerline in the Ptarmigan Creek area, Burger Shack and Black Slab offer short, relatively flat approaches for the smallest kids or older relatives and friends. Powerline, on the west side of the pass boasts 5 easy sport climbs. The Burger Shack area, near Ptarmigan Creek, provides easy routes to toprope with an even shorter hike—about two minutes. On the east side of the divide, Black Slab provides only 2 sport routes, but the approach is about a minute.

Monitor Rock, with both long multi-pitch routes and sport climbs, has the longest routes along Independence Pass. For those who want to climb a multi-pitch route and experience the thrill of reaching the top of a cliff, Monitor presents a six-pitch 5.6 outing with terrific views from the top. Numerous scenic campgrounds along a refreshing river round out the experience.

Aspen Expeditions provides guiding at several cliffs. When I was at at Powerline Cliff, one of the guides, Gabe Metzger, set up topropes for a family with their three children who came every summer from Michigan and hired Aspen guides.

## The Thumbs Up and Thumbs Down on Independence Pass...........

 **Pros:** Short approaches; beautiful scenery with abundant alpine flowers; cool in summer; interesting wildlife (marmots, beaver, deer); good quality rock; fun easy climbs; nice camping; free access; a creek tumbling down the canyon to cool off after climbing; some free camping.

 **Cons:** Mosquitoes at some of the crags; rockfall at Monitor; afternoon thundershowers.

## Climbing here is mostly...

## Logistics at a Glance

? time
Approach

On average 5 to 8 minutes, slightly uphill. Monitor Rock is steep & rocky.

Food?

Aspen is about 10-20 minutes away if climbing on West Independence & Twin Lakes is about 7 minutes away if climbing at Monitor Rock.

Rock Type

Granite and Gneiss

Cell Coverage

Not at crags. Available in Aspen and Twin Lakes.

Climb Type

Sport and Traditional Gear, 1 - 2 ropes, draws; nuts, cams on gear climbs.

Hot Spots

Provin' Grounds Coffee/Bakery 508 Harrison Ave. in Leadville

Cold Inc. Coffee 520 E Durant Ave, in Aspen (among many others..Library on Mill St.)

Ages

All ages depending on the crag (Monitor Rock over 7 best).

Dogs?

Yes, on a leash

Camping?

**East of Independence Pass**
5 USFS campgrounds, $12.00
**West of Independence Pass**
Forest Service Campgrounds and One Thousand Trails company campgrounds. See camping info.

Seasons

Summer and Early Fall

## How many routes are here?*

| Grade | Count |
|-------|-------|
| 5.0-5.6 | 6 |
| 5.7 | 14 |
| 5.8 | 30+ |
| 5.9 | 30+ |

* This statistic is for reference only, not all climbs of these grades have been chosen for this book.

GETTING
THERE

**From Boulder or Denver**, take I-70 west to the turnoff for Copper Mountain and Leadville. Drive towards Leadville on Highway 91. Pass through Leadville and continue on Highway 24 for another 13 miles to the turnoff for Highway 82 to Twin Lakes and Independence Pass. From the junction, drive about six miles to the historic hamlet of Twin Lakes where you can find several lodging options and perhaps buy essentials at the Twin Lakes General Store.

Drive six miles to Monitor Rock, the largest of the crags dotting the roadside to Aspen. At 24 miles past the junction of Highways 82 and 24 cross the continental divide over Colorado's highest paved pass, 12,095-foot Independence Pass. Driving from Twin Lakes toward the crags near Aspen takes longer than expected since the narrow windy road has numerous hairpin switchbacks and considerable traffic on summer weekends.

**From the western slope,** head east on I-70, take Exit 116 in Glenwood Springs toward CO 82, and follow the signs toward Carbondale. Continue about 40 miles and head through Aspen. Continue following signs to CO 82, turn left on Highway 24 (Independence Pass) and head up toward the crags.

Independence Pass is closed during the winter. Normally the road opens sometime around Memorial Day and closes when the snow begins to stick on the road. Head to www.cotrip.org for closures.

SETTING UP
CAMP

**East of Independence Pass**

Around the lakes, camping is permitted only in campgrounds. Several USFS campgrounds located between the lakes and the continental divide are usually open from Memorial Day until Labor Day on a first come, first serve basis. In July, the busiest month, the campgrounds fill up by Thursday for the weekend. Camping costs $12.00 per night and $5.00 for day-use, picnicking or parking.

Below is a list of Forest Service Campgrounds in the Twin Lakes area. Allo contain some first come-first serve sites, although several do allow reservaions. Most are open Memorial Day through Labor Day. See text for details.

**1. Twin Peaks Campground** – 39 sites
First come-first serve; sites cost $9.00 per night. From Twin Lakes, drive approximately 3.2 miles west on Highway 82 to the Twin Peaks Campground which offers drinking water, toilets, picnic tables, fire rings, grills, and garbage collection. The well-spaced sites lie among the aspen trees and above and along the river. We liked the layout and privacy of the sites better than at the other campgrounds. Monitor Rock is super close. Information: (719) 553-1400.

**2. Parry Peak Campground** – 26 sites

Parry Peak Campground (about 2.7 miles west of Twin Lakes Reservoir on Highway 82) operates on a first come first serve policy and costs $9 per night. The campground has water, toilets, tables, fire rings with grills, and garbage removal. Nearby climbing opportunities include Monitor Rock and Black Slab. Information: (719) 553-1400.

**3. White Star Campground** – open until September 27, 68 sites

Watch for White Star campground before reaching Twin Lakes. It lies closer to boating and swimming but further from the climbing areas. An RV dump station is available here. $10.00 a night. Takes reservations. 1-800-280-CAMP

**4. Lakeview Campground- 59 sites**

At 4.0 miles from the junction of Highways 24 and 82, a sign marks the turnoff for Lakeview Campground, which lies one mile in from Highway 82. $9.00 a night, takes reservations. 1-800-280-CAMP

SETTING UP
CAMP

## West of Independence Pass

### 1. Difficult Campground

This surprisingly nice campground close to Aspen boasts shady, spacious, widely-spaced sites nestled among the aspen and along the river. Reserve sites 1 - 22, 24, and 25; others are first come, first serve. Reservations need to be made at least 4 days in advance with a two night minimum on weekends (three nights during holiday weekends). 5 day limit. $18.00 per night for a family site.

For Reservaions:  www.recreation.gov      (877) 444-6777

The next three campgrounds together provide 26 first come-first serve sites but close right after Labor Day. Information can be found at www.fs.fed.us —navigate to Colorado, White River National Forest, and then to Aspen. Fees are generally about $16, but increase each year. If you get stumped, the Aspen Ranger District (970) 925-3445 can be helpful (no reservations).

### 2. Lost Man Campground

Lost Man Campground is straight across the road from Lost Man Trailhead. From Independence Pass drive about six miles west of the pass summit; near MM 55. Nearby climbs: Wild Rock Area.

### 3. Lincoln Gulch Campground - Six sites

Nearby climbs:  Ptarmigan Creek Area, Wild Rock.

### Lincoln Creek Road

You can camp for free along Lincoln Creek Road with a 15-day limit. Nearby climbs include Ptarmigan Creek Area and Wild Rock.

### 4. Weller Campground

Includes water, trash collection, vault toilets and firewood.

HOTELS &
MOTELS

## East of Independence Pass

**Mount Elbert Lodge**, PO Box 40, Twin Lakes, CO  81251
(719) 486-0594      www.mountelbert.com
Mount Elbert Lodge, open year-round, provides up to four-bedroom cabins with full kitchens and baths as well as B&B rooms. Continental breakfast includes hot muffins or scones, toast, juice, milk, cereal, fruit, and occasionally eggs. For dinner, the only options are eating in Buena Vista or Leadville. The lodge is often booked solid in summer. In September many visitors come to view the fall colors, so plan ahead.

HOTELS &
MOTELS

## East of Independence Pass

**Twin Lakes Roadhouse Lodge**, 6411 E. State Highway 82, Twin Lakes
(719) 486-9345    www.twinlakescolorado.com
The lodge supplies one and two bedroom cabins plus lodge rooms and is
smoke and pet free. It serves dinner for lodge guests only.

**Twin Lakes Nordic Inn**
6435 E State Highway 82, Twin Lakes
(719) 486-1830

## West of Independence Pass

**Snowmass Club**, 239 Snowmass Club Cir., Snowmass Village
(970) 923-7614    www.villasatsnowmassclub.com
If you're looking to go all out and have a more pampered experience, this
could be a good option. 1, 2 and 3 bedroom villas are available around the
golf course, but the highlight is full use of the Snowmass Athletic Club.
The kids will love the tiered stone, warm-water pools, and adults can relax
in the hot tubs and enjoy the health club.

**Little Nell**, 675 East Durant Ave., Aspen
(970) 920-4600    www.thelittlenell.com
The Little Nell allows the family dog (or cat) and even supplies dog beds
and food bowls for them. As Independence Pass allows dogs at the cliffs, this
complements your *Holiday with Rover* opportunity. Maybe it helps that Cindy
Hirschfeld, who wrote *Canine Colorado*, lives near Aspen. Pets must remain
leashed at all times. The Little Nell supplies personalized brass identification tags, food and water bowls, dog beds, pet menu selections, dog walking,
treats, and recommends groomers and pet friendly hiking trails.

**Hotel Jerome**, 330 East Main St., Aspen
(970) 920-1000    www.hoteljerome.com
The much-acclaimed Hotel Jerome provides music, videos, a CD library,
Nintendo, books, board games and videotapes for the kids. See their *Just
For Kids* page on their web site for more activities in Aspen. The dining is
supposed to be excellent as well.

## Other Aspen Lodging Options

**Websites:** www.AspenSnowmassReservations.com,
www.SkiAspenColorado.net, www.resortquest.com

**Aspen Meadow Resort**
845 Aspen Meadow Road    (970) 925-7790

**Aspen Sky Hotel**
709 E. Durant Ave.    (970) 925-6760

**Molly Gibson Lodge**
101 W. Main St.    (970) 925-3434

**The Gant - Condo Resort**
610 West End    (970) 925-5000

**The Residence Hotel**
305 South Galena St.    (970) 920-6532

SHOPPING &
GROCERIES

**Twin Lakes General Store**

6451 E. State Highway 82, Twin Lakes (719) 486-2196
The Twin Lakes General Store sells camp fuel, ice, basic groceries, camping supplies, gasoline and cold beer. They carry a large collection of souvenirs and gifts for unsuspecting tourists.

**City Market Food & Pharmacy Store**

711 E. Cooper Ave., Aspen, (970) 925-2590

**Clarks Market**

300 Puppy Smith St., Aspen, (970) 925-8046

RESTAURANTS
& COFFEE

### East of Independence Pass

Eateries in Buena Vista (25 miles away) or Leadville (23 miles) provide the closest dining on the east side of the divide. For those climbing on the west side, drive to Aspen for unlimited dining options (including some very expensive ones).

**Windspirit Cafe**

6559 Highway 82, Twin Lakes
(719) 486-8138  www.twinlakescoloradocabins.com     Open 11-4
Here you can eat a hearty lunch including burgers, sandwiches or wraps. They also sell ice cream, pack lunches and homemade pies.

### West of Independence Pass

Charlotte Fox, the renowned alpinist who's climbed the most 8,000-meter peaks of any American woman, lives in Aspen. She likes Little Annie's and the Woody Creek Tavern (10 minutes out of town in Woody Creek). The Adelman family, with three kids, said, "We love Little Annie's — great for BBQ ribs and chicken, very family friendly." They also like to eat at Johnny McGuire's and the Steak Pit.

In case you're wondering how a climber and guidebook author manages to eat at Aspen's finest restaurants – I didn't. I got these recommendations from Dave Goldstein, whose mother owns a second home in Aspen. Dave said, "When eating out in Aspen, think Manhattan, not Moab, for comparison." However, he commented that while the restaurants had great chefs that prepare 5-star food, the service does not live up to the quality of the food — waiters tend to be lift operators and other ski bums.

### Johnny McGuire's Deli

730 East Cooper Ave., Aspen, 9 am-9 pm daily
(970) 920-9255    www.johnnymcguires.com
For something reasonable, including soups, sandwiches, subs, burritos, and breakfast, try this deli. For soup lovers, it's a winner of the Soupsköl Soup Contest.

### Little Annie's Eating House

517 East Hyman, Aspen  (970) 925-1098
A great choice for some good old fashioned barby, beer and bundt cake.

### Woody Creek Tavern

2858 Woody Creek Rd,  Aspen  (970) 923-4585
Reservations not accepted.            Credit Cards not accepted.
This local hangout is one of the rare old-time, rustic taverns remaining in Aspen and was Hunter Thompson's favorite hangout. They serve outstanding tavern food, including barbecued pork ribs, steaks, burgers, fresh tilapia, organic salads, vegetarian soups, and superb Mexican food. Drive west on Colo. 82, 3/4 mile past the Snowmass Village turnoff, turn right on Smith Rd. into Woody Creek Canyon, turn left at the first fork, and continue just over a mile. This road can be icy in winter.

### Poppycock's

609 E. Cooper St., Aspen  (970) 925-1245   Breakfast & Lunch
The pancakes are so amazing that they sell the mix. Oatmeal, crepes, waffles, fruit and other breakfast standards make this a local favorite.

### Cold Inc Coffee

520 E. Durant Ave., Aspen  (970) 544-0588
Located downtown, this spot will steam your morning latte.

### Piñons Restaurant

105 South Mill Street, Aspen  (970) 920-2021    www.pinons.net
Dinners served seasonally from 5:30 until close.
Reservations accepted. Serves American food and called "extraordinary to perfection."

### Syzygy Restaurant

520 East Hyman Avenue, 2nd Floor, Aspen
(970) 925-3700  www.syzygyrestaurant.com
Reservations only. Accepted by phone. Music begins at 10 pm
Considered one of the best restaurants in Aspen, it offers Modern American food accompanied by live jazz. The menu offers a mix of French, Asian and Italian dishes, including Angus beef filet and elk tenderloin.

## What Else Can We Do That's Fun?

### Bouldering

Perkins' guidebook does an excellent job of describing the bouldering along Independence Pass as does the *Colorado Bouldering* series. Since there are so many boulder problems in this well-developed area, have a book in hand if going cordless is in your plans. For a quick fix of V0-V2, head 2.8 miles up the pass from Aspen, park at a pullout on the right, cross the highway and head up a trail to the Patrol Boulder.

### Mountain Biking

Miles of quality (some challenging) trails are located near Twin Lakes, Buena Vista, and Aspen. Benningfield's book describes six trails near Aspen and another eight in the Roaring Fork Valley. At the Twin Lakes Visitor Center you can pick up a free Mountain Bike Guide to the trails around Buena Vista and Salida. *Mountain Biking Colorado's Western Slope: The Very Best Rides from Aspen to Fruita*, Phillip Benningfield, 2000.

### Hiking

Six of Colorado's highest mountains, including 14,433-foot Mt. Elbert, surround Twin Lakes. The Colorado Trail crosses Highway 82 just west of the Mt. Elbert Power Plant, then travels along the south shore of the lakes before it heads south toward Mount Harvard.   www.coloradotrail.org

**Willis Lake:** The hike to Willis Lake and the mine past the lake is accessed from the Willis Gulch trailhead, two miles west of Twin Lakes near Parry Peak campground. A 5.5-mile hike, gaining 2,400 feet of elevation, shares the trailhead with Little Willis Gulch. From here the Colorado Trail heads over Hope Pass.

**Braille Trail:** Maureen Keilty, in her book *Best Hikes With Children in Colorado*, describes short hikes suitable for smaller children. One of these, the Braille Trail, starts on Highway 82 about 13 miles from Aspen between mile markers 53 and 54, near Powerline crag. The 0.25-mile loop at 10,400 feet, designed for blind hikers, features 22 interpretive stations which describe scents, sounds and things to feel in both Braille and print. After crossing the river on a bridge, it loops around along through the forest. The signs denote moss, different trees, and mushrooms. No toilets or water are available at the trailhead.

**Discovery Trail:** Take the baby jogger on this wheelchair trail which winds along the river passing flowers and moss. Picnic tables and benches are wheelchair-accessible. The trail begins near the start of the Braille Trail.

**The Grottos**: From Aspen, drive 10.2 miles south and pass a Forest Service campground sign. Drive 0.9 miles further and turn right just beyond a 25 mph sign. A sub-mile loop curves along fairly flat trails to a little waterfall and some small caves. Sand beaches on the river invite play in the water. Be careful of the lethal falls and rapids.

A.

B.

A. The Braille Trail
B. Twin Lakes
C. The Grottos
   (This playful cascade resembles a duck's open beak)

C.

REST DAY
ACTIVITIES

### Boating, Water and Fishing

**Twin Lakes Boat Tours**

(719) 221-9919

Take a tour of the Twin Lakes, Colorado's largest glacial lakes. Two-hour guided tours begin at the Moache Parking Area east of Twin Lakes Village. The tour stops by the historic Inter-Laken resort, an 1880s ghost town on the far shore of the lakes. The tour continues to the south shore, where ospreys nest, and around islands at the lower end of the lake.

### Canoe and Kayak Rentals:
### Twin Lakes Canoe and Kayak Adventures

(719) 251-9961

Call this outfit if you want to rent a boat on the Twin Lakes. Clear blue water sparkles below you; dark blue skies rise above.

### Rafting : Buena Vista and Aspen

Brown's Canyon, along the Arkansas River between Buena Vista and Salida, offers some of the best and most scenic whitewater around. Other stretches beckon the brave and mild. Over 30 outfitters provide half-day, full-day, and multi-day raft trips on the Arkansas.

In addition, several rafting companies based in Aspen offer trips down the Colorado River near Glenwood Springs. Give **Aspen Whitewater Rafting** a go at (970) 920-3511.

### Explore
### Independence Ghost Town

At over 10,800 feet high, this may be one of the highest ghost towns. Founded on July 4, 1879 after the discovery of gold, Independence was the first town in the Roaring Fork Valley. Later in the 1800s, the gold ran out, trains came to Aspen, and Independence lost its main function as a stagecoach stop. Some old log cabins, the general store and stables remain today.

### Twin Lakes Visitor's Center

Many buildings in Twin Lakes date to from the 1860s to 1880s after prospectors found gold and silver in 1859. The town is listed on the National Register of Historic Places and the Visitor Center is in the historic Red Rooster tavern. Prehistoric sites near the eastern end of Twin Lakes indicate that Indians lived here for thousands of years.

Madeleine Adelman
on **Dusty** 5.7

## Aspen Center for Environmental Studies

ACES at Hallam Lake, 100 Puppy Smith St., Aspen

(970) 925-5756     aces@aspennature.org

## Rock Bottom Ranch

2001 Hooks Spur Road, Basalt, CO 81621

(970) 927-6760     rockbottom@sopris.net

This environmental education center has 2 locations - the 25-acre
Hallam Lake Nature Preserve and a 113-acre Wildlife Preserve at Rock
Bottom Ranch in Basalt. Hallam Lake features a self-guided nature trail
with meadows, a pond, marsh, and many birds.

*Independence Pass Rock Climbing,* Tom Perkins, 2003.
This guide covers both climbing and bouldering along Independence Pass.
Purchase of the guidebook confers access to new route information on
their website.   www.aspenclimbingguides.com
*Rock Climbing Colorado*, Stewart Green, 1995.
*Colorado Bouldering*, Phillip Benningfield, revised 2006.
*Colorado Bouldering 2*, Benningfield and Samet, 2003.

### Hospitals

| | |
|---|---|
| **St. Vincent Hospital** | **Heart of the Rockies Medical** |
| 822 W. 4th St, Leadville | 448 E. 1st St., Salida |
| (719) 486-0230 | (719) 539-6661 |
| **St. Vincent General Hospital** | **Aspen Valley Hospital** |
| 400 Washington St., Leadville | 401 Castle Creek Rd., Aspen |
| (719) 486-1504 | (970) 925-1120 |

### Rangers

| | |
|---|---|
| **Leadville Ranger District** | **Aspen Ranger District** |
| 2015 North Poplar | 806 West Hallam |
| Leadville, CO  80461 | Aspen, CO 81611 |
| (719) 486-0749 | (970) 925-3445 |

### Guide Schools

**Aspen Expeditions**

426 S. Spring St.

Aspen, CO

(970) 925-7625

aspenexpeditions.com

To hire a guide in the Aspen area, try Aspen
Expeditions (an AMGA certified service),
which offers guided rock climbing, mountaineering, and high altitude trekking. A private
guide will cater to any group size, age or
experience level.

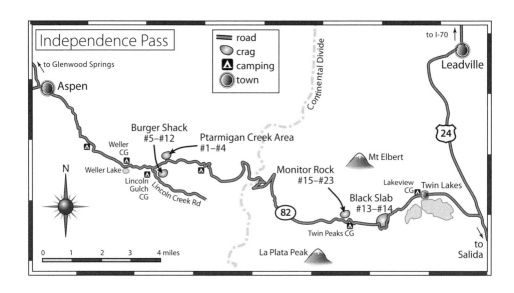

## PTARMIGAN CREEK AREA / POWERLINE

**Warning:**
Mosquitoes

**Approach:** To reach the Powerline crag from Aspen, drive 0.25 miles past mile marker 52 to a pullout directly behind the 35 mph sign. Park in the pullout on the south side of the road or turn left onto a narrow dirt road across from the pullout. Either walk or drive up the dirt road for 0.1 mile to a spot with parking for two to three cars.

A trail with cairns heads sharp left. Follow the trail, walking next to the powerlines, for two to three minutes. After crossing a talus field, the trail turns right and heads uphill to the cliff. Three fun and well-bolted beginner climbs have good anchors and a flat base. This would come close to perfection with one exception: we encountered voracious mosquitoes in July. Take bug repellent. Later in summer, after the snowmelt dries, the mosquitoes may be less rapacious.

The local guide services often bring their clients here, so the cliff may be crowded. Our first time, we had the cliff to ourselves; the second time a guide had five clients on variations of three topropes and another party was climbing on the far left end of the cliff. We got the one remaining route.

### ____1. Last 1/2 Inch 5.7 ★★

Walk toward the left side of the cliff where two climbs follow two sets of bolts. *Last 1/2 Inch* is the leftmost of the three climbs on this cliff. Follow disjointed flakes and face climbing past well-positioned bolts. At the top, two bolts with chains provide an excellent anchor for toproping. One rope easily reaches the ground. 6 clips.

### ____2. Dusty 5.7 ★★

*Dusty* follows discontinuous cracks and flakes up the face about 15 - 20 feet right of *Last 1/2 Inch.* An excellent route, it features many bolts, good rock with low-angle slab climbing and a solid anchor for rappelling or toproping. Plus, it's only 20 feet right of another great beginner's climb. 6 clips.

### ____3. Thread It Up 5.8 ★★

Walk to the right side of Powerline. Three sets of bolts lead up three slab climbs. The first of these, *Thread It Up*, lies behind the large tree. At 5.8, it offers a few moves in the bottom half that are more challenging than the two previous climbs. 6 clips, rap anchors.

### ____4a. Toe Curl 5.8 ★★

On the right side of Powerline, a second line of six bolts heads up along flakes, cracks, and face climbing. It's well bolted and on solid rock with good face holds. 6 clips.

### ____4b. Name Unknown 5.8

Just right of *Toe Curl*, a previously undocumented route follows discontinuous cracks to a bolted anchor. The first two bolts are widely spaced (though on easy ground) with potential for a long fall, followed by three bolts very close together. This climb may not be best for a beginning leader. However, if every other climb is taken, it's worth toproping. 5 clips.

**Other climbs:**
**Not Necessarily Recommended**

We climbed several routes at Greg's Cliff and Storm Jumper Wall, both in the Ptarmigan Creek Area. *Truth Decay*, rated 5.9 in Perkin's guidebook, felt more like 5.10 with its steep crux on small crimpy edges. The other routes there, *5.9 Crack* (goes at 5.10b) and *Bolts and a Pin* (also 5.10b) both felt quite stiff. The trail up to Greg's Cliff is steep with a precipitous base area that's not good for kids. Storm Jumper Wall provides a flatter base area, but with a longer hike to get to its lone 5.9 route, *Bucket Brigade*, which features large buckets albeit on a noticeably overhanging wall. Other cliffs on the Pass offer shorter approaches and easier climbs.

Isabella Adelman on *Toe Curl 5.8*

# LINCOLN CREEK: BURGER SHACK AREA
# FINGER FOOD WALL

**Approach:** From Twin Lakes, drive west for 27 miles, crossing the pass, to Lincoln Creek Road, between mile markers 52 and 51. A pullout on the right and a road on the left denote the junction. Turn left and follow the bumpy, rocky dirt road for 0.2 to 0.3 miles and park at a pullout on the right immediately before a hairpin turn in the road. The trail begins across the road from the pullout. Hike up the trail for about two minutes to where the crag appears on the left and head to the left side of the cliff, beneath the first 2 routes.

One can lead the routes described below or set up topropes. Walk to the left side of the cliff and follow an easy trail to the top of the cliff from where it's fairly simple to set topropes. Long runners on some anchors are useful for toproping. Bring a selection of stoppers and cams.

### ____5. Taco Time 5.8 ★

Ascend the left-facing corner near the left side of the crag. Start directly up the crack beneath the corner, which increases the difficulty to 5.9. Alternatively, commence 15-20 feet left of the crack, balancing up face holds which could result in a pendulum.

### ___6. Food Fight 5.7 ★

It's best to toprope this climb as few gear placements exist. *Food Fight* starts with sloping face climbing below a bulge. Climb up the face and right to a crack on the face, and then continue up a dihedral. Try several variations from the anchors: either climb straight up to the corner, try the roof on the right, or jam the crack in the corner the entire way up.

### ___7. Popsicle 5.5 ★

From the trail, look for a big alcove with an aspen behind a flake. Scramble up the left side of the alcove to reach the top. The anchors are behind the small aspen trees. To climb the route, stay left and follow the crack in the corner to the top.

### ___8. Big Mac Crack 5.7 ★

Toprope or lead *Big Mac Crack* to work on jamming and layback skills. The buttress right of *Popsicle* has a nice crack which takes stoppers, TCUs, and Camalots up to a #2. Use long draws or runners as the crack has a dogleg bend.

Tristan Hechtel on incredible Big Mack Crack 5.7 Photograph by Sibylle Hechtel

## SUNSET CANTINA

**Approach:** From the Finger Food Wall continue on the trail through the trees for another two minutes to a crag on the left. The leftmost routes on the crag are difficult to protect and are generally climbed on toprope. Walk to the top along the left side of the cliff. From here, several bolted anchors are spaced along the top of the wall. From the three anchors on the left, climb up any of a number of variations to the top. The routes further left are easier and they become harder toward the right side of the wall.

___**9.** 5.6 TR ★

From the left-most anchor, the easiest route up follows the left side of the face.

___**10.** 5.7 TR ★

From the same anchor, if one climbs a bit further right, the moves become more challenging. Ascend the wall from the next anchor to the right and climb up along the flake for a 5.8 version of the face.

___**11. Fried Brains** 5.8

*Fried Brains* is just left of the big corner that holds *All You Can Eat.* Climb left under a roof to a ledge and then continue up the face above. Some lichen and decomposed, crumbly granite on the climb.

### \_\_\_\_**12. All You Can Eat** 5.8 ★★

Ascend the obvious large dihedral in the middle of the wall. Climb one of two variations: Stay left, directly in the corner, and follow the thin 5.8 crack. Alternately, lead the corner and bear right at the small bulge and up the flake right of the corner. This variation is much easier and reaches the same two-bolt chain anchor. A bit mossy and sandy at the start, but it improves.

Tristan Hechtel on *All You Can Eat* 5.8

# BLACK SLAB

**Warning:**
Mosquitoes

**Approach:** Drive toward Parry Peak Campground. Across the street from the campground, a dirt road leads toward a quarry. Drive toward the quarry, where there are several dispersed campsites scattered among the trees. Park here and walk to the south to where Black Slab is visible. Hike uphill a short distance to the base of the cliff. The base area is relatively flat and very close to the car; the climbs are short and have bolted anchors. Black Slab is a great place to take beginners, little kids, or your favorite older friends and relatives.

### ___13. Left Route 5.7 ★

Climb up on slabby friction to the first bolt, about 20 feet off the ground, and then continue climbing on friction with occasional edges and a little moss. Since the first bolt is a bit high, this might not be the best place for a beginning leader. The anchor consists oftwo2 bolts with no chains or rappel rings. 5 clips (not 4, as in Perkin's guidebook).

### ___14. Right Route 5.9

The *Right Route* sports five bolts, four of which are bordering on antique, and the first lies about 25 feet up. Not only are the ancient bolts less than reassuring, but the rock is a little mossy in places. We traversed from the top of the *Left Route* to toprope the climb. My son thought the 5.7 was more interesting, with some edges and nubbins, whereas he found the 5.9 "just blank". Toprope from two bolts (no chains or rings).

# MONITOR ROCK

**Approach:** From Twin Lakes, drive five to six miles west, passing Parry Peak Campground. Soon after, Monitor Rock appears on the right. Park in one of two parking areas on the left. The first provides easier access to the east side, including Clairabell Mine Wall, and the second sits across from the trailhead for the main, or west wall. Beware of afternoon thunderstorms if climbing a longer route. Storms come in quickly and one can't see them coming if on the other side of the cliff. Bring ropes and draws; nuts and cams on gear climbs.

West Face Walls

A. Endless Wall
B. Ironside Wall
C. Boulder Wall

The Nose

Butt Wall

A

B

C

Trailhead Wall

## THE NOSE AND THE BUTT WALL

**Approach:** Park at the second (west) parking area and hike up the main trail. Shortly after passing a trailhead sign, a faint climber's trail branches to the right. Follow it toward the southeast ridge of Monitor Rock. The trail is fairly steep and involves some scrambling across rock bands and wouldn't be a good place to try to take a stroller or very small kids.

**___15. The Nose** 5.6 ★★

*The Nose* is an especially fun multi-pitch climb for kids or beginners. The climbing is relatively straightforward with a great view from the top. Scramble to the right side of Butt Wall. *Matillda*, the right-most bolted face climb on Butt Wall, is about 30 ft to the left of *The Nose*. To the right of *Matillda* lies a groove/corner with a small tree about 30 feet up. Follow the groove up to another larger tree on the skyline. The first pitch, on very polished rock, is the hardest pitch on the climb and may intimidate the novice 5.6 leader. Continue up the easiest cracks and grooves for four easy pitches to the top. The latter pitches offer easy low-angle climbing.

**Descent:** Walk along the top to the north end of the rock. Scramble down through trees and shrub to the west side of Monitor Rock. Alternatively, scramble down along the cliff on the east side of the rock. This descent, though circuitous, and perhaps a bit longer, involves less bushwhacking.

Tristan Hechtel on *The Nose* 5.6

# BUTT WALL

**Approach:** Hike up as for The Nose area, but instead of continuing to the right, head uphill to the polished wall ahead with a treed alcove.

### ___16. Little Flatulence 5.8 ★

Look for the first line to the right of the alcove. Ascend right to the base to belay. Follow the line of bolts up to an anchor. The rock here is very polished, reminiscent of the glacier polish in Tuolomne Meadows, but the incut holds are positive and there when needed. Three bolts provide an anchor, but no chains or rings are present. 9 clips.

### ___17. Going Greek 5.9 ★★

While up here, climb the two 5.9 face routes that start, respectively, about 20 and 40 feet left of *Little Flatulence*. *Going Greek* starts in a gully

directly left of a large tree. The first two bolts have old, homemade hangers and the next nine bolts are cold shuts. *Going Greek* has some polished rock, but not as much as *Little Flatulence*. Three bolts await at the top, again lacking chains and rings. 11 clips.

### ___18. Left Cheek 5.9 ★

Scramble up to a ledge with a tree above and left of the gully from which the previous line starts. This climb resembles *Going Greek*, with its smooth rock and incut face holds. My son thought that *Going Greek* was the more interesting of the two climbs, but Tom Perkins gives only *Left Cheek* a smiley face. For these two climbs, a 60-meter rope reaches the gully. A 55-meter rope reaches as far as the ledge with the tree, and you can scramble down from here. 9 clips.

## WEST SIDE ROUTES

**Warning:** Possible rock fall

**Approach:** To reach the west side walls, continue straight on the main trail rather than turning right toward the Butt Wall. The first wall you come to, where the trail reaches the rock, is the Trailhead Wall. From here, head left and uphill. After a few minutes, the trail starts weaving between big boulders and then continues on into a talus field. The Ironside Wall is on the right.

___**19. Baby Doe** 5.8 ★★★
*Baby Doe* heads up the prow on the very right edge of the wall. Start beside a little tree and traverse right to the first bolt and then continue straight up on face holds. *Baby Doe* is an easy well-bolted 5.8 with no scary runouts. 6 clips.

## BOULDER WALL

The Boulder Wall lies a short way uphill from where the main trail hits the Trailhead Wall. Look for two large trees and a wall with a dihedral on each side. The two dihedrals are easy but require gear. Both lack anchors but from the left dihedral one can traverse to the anchor of *Grave Line* and set up a toprope.

___**20. Grave Line** 5.10a ★
*Grave Line* begins about five ft right of the lefthand dihedral. The direct start, straight up to the bolt, is tricky, polished, pumpy, and insecure. I climbed up the corner and traversed right to reach the first bolt, as I'm not overly fond of ground falls. After the start, the rest of the route consists of pleasant face climbing on small edges. 7 clips.

# IRONSIDE WALL

### ____21. Prospector 5.10a

*Prospector* is six routes left of *Baby Doe* and goes over (or around) a small roof. Going over the roof is pumpy and footholds feel slippery. Above the roof the route provides intricate face climbing. The anchor is equipped with two chains. 7 clips.

### ____22. Twin Flakes 5.10b ★★

The second climb left of *Prospector* follows a prominent left-angling dihedral. A chain at the second bolt makes it easier for short climbers to clip the bolt prior to the hard moves. We found *Twin Flakes* easier than *Prospector*, which has a strenuous move over a roof. *Twin Flakes* has no single move as pumpy but remains continuously interesting. 8 clips.

## ENDLESS WALL

**Approach**: Walk uphill from the Ironside Wall and pass the huge left-facing corner. The corner itself is a 5.9 gear climb. To the left of the corner are two nice 5.10 sport climbs. Perkins warns that climbs on this wall are harder for their grade than some other climbs at Monitor Rock.

### ___23. Printer Boy 5.10a ★

I'm not sure whether this falls into the "harder 10a" category or not, but the start seems a bit stout. It's a really enjoyable climb that has a hard second pitch. There's a tricky move at bolt seven, which short climbers cannot clip prior to doing the crux move. I'm 5'7" and just barely reached the bolt to clip, so be prepared.

Tristan Hechtel on *Baby Doe* 5.8

Tristan Hechtel on **How the West Was Won** 5.10a

Photograph by Sibylle Hechtel

# PENITENTE CANYON

If you're looking for an excellent cragging destination to take little kids, don't miss Penitente Canyon in the San Luis Valley. It's one of the few places where a jogging stroller can make the journey to the crag. With one of the shortest and flattest approaches anywhere, great campsites, and even a 5.2 climb, Penitente scores high in family-friendliness.

The area includes Penitente Canyon and the adjacent Rock Garden, Sidewinder and Witches Canyons, but Penitente hosts the greatest concentration of easy climbs. The rock here resembles Hueco Tanks—a volcanic tuff that formed 33 million years ago when volcanoes covered the land with ash up to 1,800 feet deep. Heat and pressure turned this ash into rock, which eroded, cracked and rounded at the edges, to form strange shapes and unusual climbing formations.

The San Luis Valley is the world's largest alpine valley, with an average altitude of 7,500 feet. An amazing campground in piñon-covered grassland welcomes visitors at the entrance to the canyon. Camping is first come, first serve at this time and doesn't require reservations. Generally dry weather permits climbing from spring through fall, but the high altitude (nearly 8,000 ft) creates chilly nights. The same welded tuff that forms the climbs of Penitente Canyon also shaped boulders covering the surrounding hills which provide excellent bouldering.

View from the campground toward the San Luis Valley and the Sangre de Cristo Mounains, with San Juan Art Center in the sun.

## The Thumbs Up and Thumbs Down on Penitente Canyon.............

 **Pros:** Very short approaches; nice camping; gorgeous scenery; relatively safe for kids; dogs permitted on leash.

 **Cons:** Can be crowded on weekends; not many easy climbs; remote from large cities; rattlesnakes.

## Climbing here is mostly...

## Logistics at a Glance

| | | | | |
|---|---|---|---|---|
|  Approach | 5-10 Minutes | |  Food? | Limited offerings at nearby La Garita Cash Store. |
|  Rock Type | Volcanic Tuff | |  Cell Coverage | No Access |
|  Climb Type | Sport | |  Hot Spots | No Wireless Internet |
|  Ages | Any age. Older or disabled climbers OK, due to flat approach. | |  Dogs? | Yes |
|  Camping? | $5 a night, first-come first-serve basis. No water on site. See text for more details. | |  Seasons | Spring and Fall are best. Summer could be OK but tends to be hot. |

## How many routes are here?*

| **Penitente Canyon** | 5.0-5.6 | 1 |
|---|---|---|
| | 5.7 | 1 |
| | 5.8 | 2 |
| | 5.9 | 2 |

\* This statistic is for reference only, not all climbs of these grades have been chosen for this book.

GETTING
THERE

Take Highway 285 south for 17.2 miles from Saguache to G Road. Watch for signs for T, S and R roads. Turn right (west) on G road at sign for La Garita and follow this for 5.4 miles to La Garita. From La Garita, continue heading west for about 1.4 miles. Bear left at the first minor junction and look for a sign steering you right toward Penitente Canyon. Drive about 0.6 miles to a junction parking and camping. To camp, head another 0.3 miles up or continue straight for trailhead parking. Walking from the campsites to the trailhead may be advisable on busy weekends when the parking area fills up.

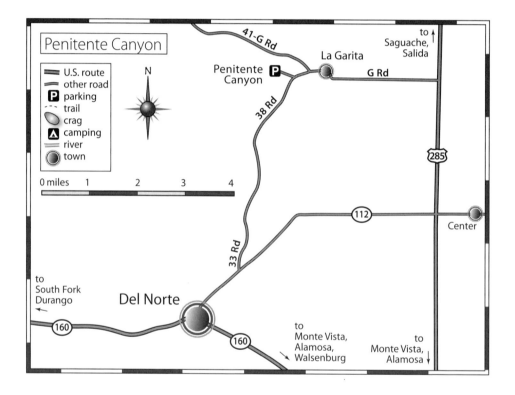

SETTING UP
CAMP

The BLM provides two campgrounds, a lower one with larger group sites and RV sites, and a higher one on the lefthand road with individual sites. They charge $5 per night and do not require reservations (but if you get there on a busy Saturday, you may not find a site). The sites provide comfortable sand-filled tent platforms, picnic tables, vault toilets, and trash removal, but no water at this time (There is a sign with a water icon just outside the canyon as you head toward La Garita). The sites are nicely spread out among the piñon trees, allowing some privacy.
GPS: 13S 0386965 UTM 4188956        Alt: 8,000 ft

HOTELS &
MOTELS

**The La Garita Ranch**, a Bed and Breakfast about four miles from Penitente, welcomes climbers. You'll find some great bouldering nearby.
38145 County Road 39, Del Norte, CO 81132
(888) 838-3833    (719) 754-2533

**Del Norte** (about 13 miles away) offers several hotels and motels.

SHOPPING &
GROCERIES

The **La Garita Cash Store** sells food, gas, and oil.
Hours are: Tu – F (7 – 6)    Sat (7 – 5)    Sun (7 – 3)    Closed on Monday

**The Phillips 66** (also called 1st Stop) in Saquache sells propane.

RESTAURANTS
& COFFEE

Breakfast or lunch is available at the La Garita Cash Store. For dinner,
drive to Center, Del Norte or Monte Vista. For slightly better food (but a
longer drive) head to Alamosa, about an hour's drive through Monte Vista.

### Del Norte

**Peace Of Art Cafe**
14475 US Highway 160
(719) 657-3223
Serves organic food
and drinks with friendly
service.

**Country Family Inn**
1050 Grand Ave.
(719) 657-3581

They serve a variety of
sandwiches and pastas
plus all the non-alco-
holic beverages you can
drink.

**Boogies Restaurant**
410 Grand Ave.
(719) 657-2903

### Monte Vista

**Hunan Chinese
Restaurant**
819 1st Avenue
(719) 852-2002

**Nino's**
118 Adams Street
(719) 852-0101
Serves decent Mexican
food.

### Alamosa

**Calvillo Restaurants**
400 Main St.
(719) 587-5500

**East West Grill**
408 4th St.
(719) 589-4600
Nice rice bowls!

**Hunan Chinese
Restaurant**
419 Main Street
(719) 589-9002

# What Else Can We Do That's Fun?

BOULDERING

### Bouldering

The same volcanic activity that formed the cliffs of Penitente Canyon also created myriads of boulders scattered around the San Luis Valley. You'll notice endless boulders as you pull into the main parking area (popular with the 4-year old crowd). Simply head down the climbers' trail and pan left and right for options. A couple of popular problems exist on the large boulder which faces the Virgin. Benningfield's *Colorado Bouldering* should be consulted for problem names and grades.

MOUNTAIN
BIKING

### Zapata Falls

Take Highway 150 south of Great Sand Dunes to Zapata Falls. Look for the access to Zapata Falls between mile marker 10 and 11; turn east. Look for the "Zapata Falls Recreation Area" sign and continue 3.5 miles from the turnoff. Follow the dirt road to a parking lot, picnic area, exhibits, and an accessible restroom. Pass the first pullout and after another mile, park at the second pullout. The Zapata Falls Trail offers four separate numbered loops, including 10 miles of singletrack. You can do a loop that includes sections of all four loop trails, or ride only one or two.

> **Sibylle's Travels**
> **Mountain Biking Reference**
>
> *Mountain Bike America: Colorado*
> *An Atlas of Colorado's Greatest Off-Road Bicycle Rides*, Stephen Hlawaty, 2000.
>
> Of Hlawaty's 49 best rides number 32, Zapata Falls, tours the San Luis Valley and the Great Sand Dunes. What I like about this ride is the fact that it's technically and physically easy with little elevation gain (it's the descent that bothers me more).

### Penitente Canyon

If you have older kids and they're pretty skilled on a mountain bike, explore some moderately technical terrain straight from the tent. At the information kiosk the climbing trail heads right, but if you bike out left a 4.5 mile trail heads up and rides the rim of the canyon in a clockwise direction. It descends down to the Penitente Canyon entrance road fairly close to where the trail began. Apparently endless riding is available with several spurs heading onto BLM land.

### Sand Dunes Swimming Pool

A local hot spot, these springs just north of Hooper on Hwy 17 provide some great R&R year-round. Take a dip, enjoy the views of the Sangre de Cristos, grab some grub from the snack bar, take a shower, and cruise back to your tent a happy, clean camper. Call for current hours and prices.
www.sanddunespool.com   (719) 378-2807

REST DAY
ACTIVITIES

### Alamosa - Monte Vista National Wildlife Refuge

In March and October, sandhill cranes migrate and a few rare whooping cranes usually accompany the thousands of sandhill cranes during these spectacular migrations. Mallards, pintail, teal, Canada geese, avocets, killdeer, and ibis, plus egrets and herons also can be seen here.
9383 El Rancho Lane, Alamosa, (719) 589-4021   www.fws.gov/alamosa

REST DAY
ACTIVITIES

**Sibylle's Travels**
**Great Reference**

*Best Hikes With Children in Colorado,* Maureen Keilty

• Dunes Exploration hike, a 0.3 – 0.4-mile one-way walk, drive 0.3 miles north from the visitor center and turn left. From here, cross Medano Creek and play in the dunes!

• The Montville Nature Trail, a 0.5-mile loop, starts in the same place. From the parking lot, Montville Trail skirts Mosca Creek and meets the Mosca Pass Trail where it crosses the creek.

OTHER
CLIMBING
GUIDES

EMERGENCY
INFO
&
MORE

### Great Sand Dunes National Park and Preserve

The biggest sandbox in the West, both kids and adults love to play in these dunes. When my son was little, we came here after climbing in Penitente. After scrambling up a dune, he slid, rolled and somersaulted down the dunes. In spring Medano Creek flows along the base of the dunes, creating a sand beach near some of most spectacular scenery in Colorado.

A four to five mile one-way hike leads to Star Dune, the tallest dune in North America (750 feet from base to top). Prepare for lots of sun and a bit of wind. Camp on a first come basis, with about 100 sites available. Water and bathrooms make the experience more cush.
(719) 378-6300   www.nps.gov/grsa

**From Penitente** head back to La Garita and take Hwy. 285 south to Road 5 east until you hit Hwy. 17. Take a quick jog left here (Mosca Area) and take a right on Rd 6 east (look for signs to the Dunes). Finally a left on Hwy. 150 will bring you to the park.

**From Alamosa** take Hwy. 160 for 26 miles to Highway 150. Drive another 19 miles to the park entrance and visitor center.

### San Luis Lakes State Park

View migratory waterbirds and other birds that frequently visit the lakes. Also find coyotes, kangaroo rats, rabbits, elk, raptors, reptiles, and amphibians in the riparian habitat among the dunes of the San Luis Valley.
(719) 378-2020     www.parks.state.co.us/Parks/SanLuis

*Rock Climbing Colorado*, Stewart Green, 1995.
*Rock Climbing Colorado's San Luis Valley*, Bob D'Antonio, 1999.
*Colorado Bouldering*, Phillip Benningfield, revised 2006.
*Colorado Bouldering 2*, Phillip Benningfield and Matt Samet, 2003.
*Colorado Front Range Bouldering, Volume 3: Southern Areas*, Bob Horan, 1995.

**Del Norte**
Rio Grande Hospital
1280 Grand Ave., Del Norte
(719) 657-2510

**Los Caminos Antiguos**
**Historic and Scenic Byway**
www.loscaminos.com

**Del Norte Public Library**
790 Grand Ave., Del Norte
(719) 657-2633

**BLM**
46525 Hwy. 114
Saguache
(719) 655-2547

**Center Branch Library**
400 S. Worth St., Center, CO
(719) 754-3156

## PENITENTE ROUTES

**Approach**: From the kiosk and gazebo at the parking area, walk straight east on the trail for about five minutes to a large alcove with slabby rocks just before a side canyon branches off to the right (east). On the right a very low angle slab with four bolts, *Mr. Breeze* (#4), is an excellent 5.2 climb well suited for beginners.

Parking area GPS: 8019 ft    13S 0386633 UTM 4189425

 Rattlesnakes

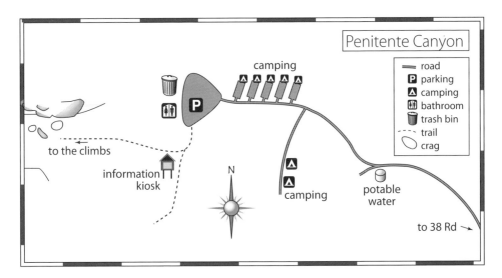

Fred and Tanner Knapp march through the Great Sand Dunes National Park    Photo by Heidi Knapp

___**1. How the West Was Won** 5.10a ★★★

From *Mr. Breeze*, continue another 75 – 100 ft to where a side canyon branches off right. Walk right (east) up the canyon for one to two minutes until almost to the end. Left of the trail on a southwest-facing wall, a climb goes up nice huecos along the left arête.

Start on huecos and pockets below the first bolt then move slightly left at the first bolt and continue up the left edge of the arête. A chance to climb on huecos doesn't occur often in Colorado hence I'm including several somewhat harder climbs.

The first bolt is about 25 ft up so bring a long stick clip or a fearless leader (I brought my 14-year old son). 3 clips.
GPS: 13S 0386659 UTM 4189478

### Routes Featured
1. How the West Was Won 5.10a
2. Captain America 5.10a
3. Maybe Nueve 5.8+ - 5.9-
4. Mr. Breeze 5.2
5. Mr. Wind 5.7
6. The Serpent 5.8
7. What the Hey 5.9+
8. Ya-Ta-Hei 5.10c

### ____2. Captain America 5.10a ★★

*Captain America* provides great climbing on huecos after surmounting the first hard move off the ledge. *Captain America* starts high off the ground after scrambling up to a ledge and thus is not a safe place to bring little kids; nor would it be an easy place to take the grandparents. It's great fun for capable climbers though. 3 clips.

### ____3. Maybe Nueve 5.8+ or 5.9- ★

On the main trail, head toward the rock just left of *Mr. Breeze*. Refer to the photo on the previous page for identification.

Start up the left side of a prominent flake about 10 feet left of an incipient crack. Ascend a few feet and then step across to the right side of the flake. Continue up the right side of the flake to reach the crack. Jam the crack for a few feet and then step right across to horizontal footholds atop a flake. From here either climb up the face left of the seam (following the line of bolts) or, for somewhat easier climbing, meander to the right of the bolts using the thin crack.

The first bolt is about 25 feet off the ground, but the friction climbing up the slab is fairly easy. Large, round bolts on this climb can be threaded to lower off if necessary.

When setting up a toprope, don't clip the bolts on the route. This will allow climbers to choose either the bolt line or the escape right on easier ground. 4 clips.

### ____4. Mr. Breeze 5.2 ★★★

The direct start to this climb—straight up to the bolt from the ground—is difficult. Instead chimney up for a few feet between *Mr. Breeze* and the rock to the right then traverse left on easy face holds. The rest of the climb offers pleasant friction climbing on a low-angle slab. Toprope from the anchor and let the kids and grandparents give it a try! As always leave in a directional to avoid pendulums.

### ____5. Mr. Wind 5.7 ★★

As with *Mr. Breeze*, a direct start provides the biggest obstacle to success. Avoid this by chimneying and stemming up between the *Mr. Wind* formation and the rock just right. Continue up the crack to the right clipping the first two to three bolts and then traverse left onto face holds. The rest of the climb, up good flakes on a low-angle slab, is easier. From this anchor, you can also let everyone try the route on toprope.

Tristan Hechtel on *Mr. Wind*

183

### ___6. The Serpent 5.8 ★★★

As with the preceding two climbs a direct start presents the most difficulty. Randy Emmons, father of the phenom Megan Emmons, (who lead 5.13 at age 11) told me he thinks the direct start is 5.10. I always thought it was pretty difficult, but didn't really want to say that for fear of being thought a wimp! Avoid it by traversing in on face holds from the right. This way is easier, but make sure you spot the leader and topropers as well. After passing the first bolt, friction up to the flat ledge where the climbing changes from low-angle slab to steeper face climbing on good edges with well-placed bolts. The leader should unclip the protection bolts when lowering, so that topropers have the option of starting further right on easier terrain.

Greg Brown on Maybe Nueve 5.8+/5.9-                    Photograph by Sibylle Hechtel

## MEGAN'S STORY

When autumn comes, and I find myself back in the monotonous pace of school, Penitente it is the perfect place to get away from everything and just climb. Rarely crowded during the week, I have my choice of any of the 250 or so technical routes scattered along the light-brown volcanic cliffs. The mild approach is especially luring this time of year as small clumps of aspens shed their golden leaves and choke cherry bushes line the narrow canyon with their reddish-orange. The cool weather, gorgeous views, and the enjoyable, balance-oriented routes, allow me to relax.

Penitente Canyon is my home climbing crag; it is where I learned to love climbing. Each time I get on one of the short routes, generally only five or six bolts long, I'm reminded of the simplicity and pure joy of movement. The nature of the rock (slightly less-than-vertical, small edges or minute shallow pockts) emphasizes technical movement and footwork, rather than brute strength.

With these unique features Penitente developed and refined my fundamental climbing skills. When I started climbing, I would toprope a route and then down climb it. Each route has so many different moves, I still

set up an anchor and climb every possible line; I spend whole afternoons on a single route. At Penitente I can struggle on 5.13s or focus on technique with pleasant 5.9s or 5.10s.

Megan Emmons

The most popular non-climbing feature of this enchanting crag is the painting of the Virgin on a starkly beautiful, red, smoothly angling wall near the center of the main canyon. The bolted line *Virgin No More* just to the right of the painting was my first project; the route was so visually appealing. At the time, it was rated 5.13a. A pocket on it was later "drilled", lowering the rating to 12+. The justification for destroying the route was for smaller climbers to enjoy it. I was just ten years old when I climbed it. I didn't see the need for altering the route at that time, and today I still don't.

I remember working the route on toprope six years ago. My crux wasn't where adults would have trouble. About 1/3 of the way up the route two pockets are spaced fairly far apart. My arms weren't long enough to reach the second pocket! It took me several tries to find a balancey sequence for gaining the second pocket. I had to go to the right, work up on thin edges, and cut back left. Once I cleanly toproped the route, with my several additional moves, I decided to lead the route. It was certainly an interesting decision, since I had never led a single route before.

The first half of the route went quite well. I repeated my delicate sequence of moves to reach the second pocket and then climbed upward to where the climb became slightly overhanging. Suddenly, I was in trouble. While running the route on toprope, I never worried about being steady enough to clip the bolts. This time it was different —very different. I couldn't get balanced long enough to clip! I climbed around and around the bolt just hoping to find a steady position. I made several strenuous passes before I was finally able to lock-off and clip. Compared to clipping that bolt, even my crux seemed easy! After only a few more technical

### ___7. What the Hey 5.9+

This is the leftmost of a trio of slabby face climbs (on the left is *What the Hei*, *Ya–Ta-Hey* is in the middle, and *That's the Way* is on the right) located before reaching *Mr. Breeze*. Following the bolt line directly creates a difficult start, but options exist to avoid this. Either climb the chimney to the right of the bolts, or stem up the corner left of the bolts. Careful, we saw a pigeon's nest when we climbed there and pigeons flying in your face at the start can be startling. Stem up the corner to about the level of the second bolt then move right onto the face. *What the Hey* gets fairly run-out in the middle section, but the climbing is reasonable. The top is thin and a bit tricky for 5.9+. 4 clips.

### ___8. Ya-Ta-Hei 5.10c ★★

*Ya-Ta-Hei* goes up the steep slab right of the chimney. Again, the start is bouldery and strenuous straight up but avoidable by stemming up the chimney at the beginning. One of the best 5.10s in the canyon, it's worth doing if you're comfortable leading at this grade.

 Not Recommended:
**Ordinary People** 5.9
This route is not featured in this book, but if you reference another guide, this is a slimy runout slab climb with big fall potential. A very hard start on polished rock adds to the unplesantness.

cruxes I reached the anchors. I remember the sense of accomplishment I felt upon placing the rope in the second draw.

It saddens me to think that no climbers will be able to climb that route and feel the same sense of purity I felt, because someone thought short people deserved a chance. I know I didn't need help; I did it on my own.

Penitente is my home; I've taken the skills learned here with me on climbing adventures across the Western Hemisphere. Penitente prepared me for long alpine climbs in the Wind River Range and the Tetons. Skill at climbing slabs enabled me to ascend runout climbs in Yosemite. Knowing I could trust my feet and balance has enabled me to climb the big, icy mountains of the Andes. For me, Penitente was a wonderful place to learn how to climb; let it do the same for generations to come. And yes, I still go there as much as possible after school!

Megan Emmons

Sibylle Fechtel on **Beginner's Luck** 5.7          Photograph by Tristan Hechtel

# UNAWEEP

Want to climb beautiful granite cracks in sunny serene mountains? Climbing at Lumpy Ridge would be fine except that the four-year old won't hike 45 minutes. Besides, it storms by noon every day in Estes Park. So where to go instead?

Unaweep has it all—clean granite cracks in gorgeous tranquil surroundings. My son, who sometimes complained about the hike to Lumpy Ridge, tolerated the 10-minute approach. Unaweep enjoys much milder and drier weather than many Front Range climbing areas. A location in Colorado's only wine-producing area makes it possible to tour wineries on non-climbing days. Free primitive camping abounds in the piñon-juniper forests where the kids can chase lizards and roast marshmallows at night. On a rest day, they can dig for dinosaur bones. A 14-year old found a dinosaur egg in the Mygatt-Moore quarry during a Family Dino Camp session run by the Dinosaur Discovery Museum.

The Sunday Wall and Lower Mothers Buttress provide short approaches coupled with short easy routes, many of which have bolted toprope anchors. If you enjoy the canyon, Baum's guidebook describes over 15 additional cliffs but few offer an abundance of one-pitch routes that can be easily toproped.

# *SERIOUS PLAY*

## *AN ANNOTATED GUIDE TO*
## *TRADITIONAL FRONT RANGE CLASSICS 5.2-5.9*

This remarkable book bridges the gap between guidebook and instructional manual. Covering the major traditional climbing venues of Colorado's Front Range, artist Steve Dieckhoff's detailed "topos" provide route information as well as descriptions of the skills and techniques needed to master the routes.

A traditional climbing *must-have* for your library

## The Thumbs Up and Thumbs Down on Unaweep.......................

 **Pros:** Beautiful location; free camping on flat BLM land in the piñon –juniper forest with hummingbirds and lizards; free firewood; dogs permitted; good bouldering; reasonable approaches.

 **Cons:** Primitive camping lacks amenities and sits above cliffs; cacti near base of climb; rockfall, vehicle (hunters) traffic in fall. The hike up to the climbs may be too steep for the oldest climbers. Campsites are close to the tops of some cliffs so keep an eye on younger children.

## Climbing here is mostly...

## Logistics at a Glance .........................................

**Approach**

10 minutes & steep
Older or disabled climbers: uphill approach, need to climb over the fence to reach the trail.

**Food?**

Grand Junction isn't too far away.

**Rock Type**

Granite and Gneiss

**Cell Coverage**

None at climbs or camping. Reception about 9 miles away toward Whitewater.

**Climb Type**

Mostly Traditional Climbing, Some multi-pitch, bring 2 ropes, nuts and cams.

**Hot Spots**

Main St. Bagels - Sixth & Main
Library - only at main branch
530 Grand Ave, Grand Junction

**Ages**

Best for ages 7 and up

**Dogs?**

Yes

**Camping?**

Free BLM camping near Unaweep. See camping details.

**Seasons**

Spring and Fall (Summer is OK but can be hot).

## How many routes are here?*

| Sunday Wall | |
|---|---|
| 5.0-5.6 | 1 |
| 5.7 | 3 |
| 5.8 | 4 |
| 5.9 | 5 |

| Lower Mother Butress | |
|---|---|
| 5.0-5.6 | |
| 5.7 | 1 |
| 5.8 | 4 |
| 5.9 | 2 |

* This statistic is for reference only, not all climbs of these grades have been chosen for this book.

**GETTING THERE**

From Grand Junction, drive south towards Delta for about nine miles on Highway 50 toward Whitewater. Turn west (right) on Highway 141 toward Gateway. Continue up the canyon for about 14 miles to the Divide Road turn-off. At a sign that says "National Forest Access, Divide Road – Uncompahgre Plateau" either turn left to camp or continue straight to the climbs.

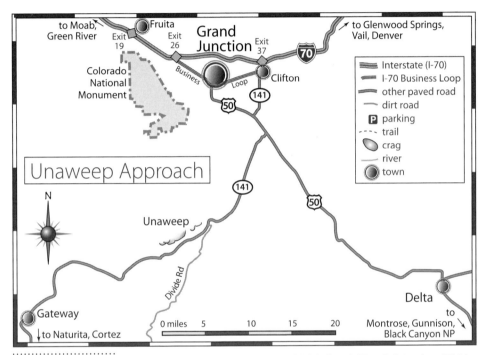

**SETTING UP CAMP**

Camp for free on BLM land along Divide Road. Turn left (east) on Divide road about 14 miles past Whitewater then drive 2.1 miles up Divide Road and cross a cattle guard. A sign states that the state provides no winter maintenance on Divide Road from October 15 to June 1. Just past the cattle guard are several sites nestled in the trees right of the road. Though these flat treed campsites provide great views they offer no water, toilets, tables or trash cans. Across the road, the BLM provides a firewood collection area. Please be sure to leave the sites clean.

GPS: Altitude: 6,901 ft        12S0710160 UTH 4300763

**HOTELS & MOTELS**

The two hotels listed below are both just off of I-70 on a freeway exit, Horizon Drive. Since they're close together, if you don't like the looks of one, it's not far to the other inn.

**Residence Inn / Marriott**, 767 Horizon Dr., Grand Junction, CO
(970) 263-4004    www.marriott.com/GJTRI
If you want to spoil yourself, enjoy luxurious bedding, kitchens, wireless internet access and work areas. The kids may enjoy the indoor pool and hot tub while you work out in the fitness room. A full complimentary hot breakfast is served daily.

**Motel 6**, 776 Horizon Dr.
Grand Junction, CO    (970) 243-2628
Spartan but cheap. No ammenities.

**SHOPPING & GROCERIES**

**City Market Food & Pharmacy**, 569 32 Rd., Clifton, CO
(970) 434-9603
The City Market near the junction of Highway 6 and 32 Road (in the Coronado Plaza) has a great salad bar. From the Clifton exit, go past the junction for Highway 50 and turn right at the next light. Fill up with gas before heading up to the Uncompahgre plateau.

**Safeway**, 681 Horizon Pl., Grand Junction, CO
(970) 254-0227

**Mt. Garfield Fruit & Vegetable Stand**, 3371 US Hwy. 6, Clifton, CO
(970) 434-7906
In August and September, numerous fruit stands sell farm fresh produce and great peaches. I've also bought terrific roasted chilies that go well in burritos and even pasta.

**Summit Canyon Mountaineering**, 461 Main Street, Grand Junction, CO
(970) 243-2847

**RESTAURANTS & COFFEE**

**Rockslide Brewery**, 401 Main St., Grand Junction, CO
(970) 245-2111
Check out this brewpub for dinner after climbing on a hot day!

**Suehiro Japanese Restaurant**, 541 Main St, Grand Junction
(970) 245-9548
A Japanese restaurant in Grand Junction? That's what we thought. But a local climber recommended it, so we went there to eat dinner. One of our party, who had been to Japan pronounced the décor quite authentic. My son enjoyed the Teriyaki vegetables and I had Sushi; we were delightfully surprised by the quality of the food.

# What Else Can We Do That's Fun?

BOULDERING

## Bouldering

Colorado Bouldering author Phillip Benningfield suggests that Unaweep Canyon may contain the largest concentration of boulder problems in the state. We found the sandstone bouldering to be a welcome change from strenuous granite cracks. For complete descriptions of boulder problems:
*Colorado Bouldering*, Phillip Benningfield, revised 2006.
*Colorado Bouldering 2*, Phillip Benningfield & Matt Samet, 2003.

Most of the bouldering sits along the side of Highway 141, heading from Whitewater up to Divide Road. Mileages below are from the intersection of Highway 50 and Highway 141.

Rock Garden is 4.3 miles on the left.
Bone Park is 5.0 miles on the right.
Hole in One Boulder is 5.8 miles on the left.
Black Wave/Brain is 7.1 miles on the right.

Tristan Hechtel on Fossil Boulder V1

**Onward**

### Colorado National Monument

Maureen Keilty, in her book *Best Hikes With Children in Colorado,* describes three great trails which lie near Grand Junction. The Trail Through Time, located 30 miles west of Grand Junction, comprises a 1.2-mile loop through a quarry with dinosaur fossils. Take I-70 west for 30 miles to the Rabbit Valley Exit (Exit 2) and follow signs to the trailhead. Trail brochures and signs describe paleontological sites along the trail.

Keilty also recommends two trails in the Colorado National Monument. Take I-70 west for 12 miles to the Fruita Exit, Exit 19. Follow Hwy 340 to Colorado National Monument and continue to the visitor center. The 0.5-mile trail Alcove Nature Trail sits across from the visitor center. An interpretive trail with 31 sites, it introduces the kids to desert plants and animals. The next trails, the Canyon Rim and Window Rock Trails, start down the stairs behind the visitor center from where one can catch a glimpse of Independence Monument and views of the Book Cliffs.

MOUNTAIN
BIKING

### Fruita: Mountain Biking Destination

Fruita is rapidly developing a reputation as a mountain bike mecca on par with Moab. The two guidebooks below cover local trails. On the famous Kokopelli Trail it's possible to ride all the way from Grand Junction to Moab, Utah.

In early May, the Fruita Fat Tire Festival starts off the mountain bike racing season with live music and a big party. If you're planning to mountain bike, don't miss the Chutes and Ladders or Lions and Troy Built Trails.
www.fruitamountainbike.com

*Mountain Biking Colorado's Western Slope: The Very Best Rides From Aspen to Fruita.* Phillip Benningfield, 2000.
*Mountain Biking Grand Junction and Fruita, 2nd edition.* Bob D'Antonio, 2002.
*Mountain Bike America: Colorado: An Atlas of Colorado's Greatest Off-Road Bicycle Rides,* Stephen Hlavaty, 2000.

REST DAY
ACTIVITIES

### Rafting and Float Trips

Rimrock Adventures, (970) 858-9555
One mile south of Fruita on Highway 340
www.rradventures.com

Colorado boasts rafting on many great rivers - the Blue, the Arkansas, Clear Creek, the Eagle, the Gunnison, the Dolores and the Colorado River. If it's too hot to climb try a day of rafting to cool off.

### Horseback Riding

Rimrock Adventures guides horseback rides in the Colorado Canyons National Conservation Area and in the Little Bookcliff Wild Horse Preserve, which covers over 30,000 acres, north of Grand Junction. A highlight of the trip is travelling into the badlands to search for wild mustangs. Rimrock Adventures also offers pony rides for smaller children.

### Colorado National Monument

Take the Fruita exit off I-70 and follow signs to the entrance. This monument is Colorado's version of the Utah desert, complete with balanced rocks, hoodoos, arches and red rock spires. Nearby Rattlesnake Canyon boasts more arches than any locale except Arches National Park. The park's Rim Rock Drive provides a showcase driving tour. (970) 858-3617

### Cross Orchards Historic Farm

3073 F Road, Grand Junction, (970) 434-9814

At this historic apple orchard, tour a farm with animals, a blacksmith and a picnic area. The country store sells gifts and local food.

### Grand Mesa National Forest

Grand Mesa is the largest flattop mountain in the world and holds 300 stream-fed lakes for fishing, hiking, cross-country skiing and hunting. We climbed in Unaweep on a May weekend when it was 94 degrees in town and fled to snow and cooler temperatures at Grand Mesa in the afternoon. (970) 242-8211    www.fs.fed.us/r2/gmug

### Vineyards

The Grand Valley is Colorado's wine country—and after a hard day of climbing adults may wish to taste the region's offerings! My friend Thomas Walsh, who teaches wine tasting, says the Colorado wine country resembles the excellent high mountain vineyards of Argentina and the wines of the two regions are similar. He recommends trying the Garfield Estates Cabernet Franc, the Debeque Syrah and Malbec, and the S. Rhodes Pinot Noir.

Reeder Mesa Vineyards, 7799 Reeder Mesa Road, Whitewater, CO (970) 242-7468, ReederMesaWines@aol.com

### National Scenic Byways

The Colorado Scenic and Historic Byways Commission designated 21 spectacular roads with scenic, historic, recreational or cultural value. Drive one of these to reach Unaweep. SH 141 and 145, a 138-mile section, passes from Whitewater through Unaweep Canyon to the Dolores River Canyon and to Placerville. A second scenic byway, SH 65 or Lands End Road, lies between I-70 and Cedaredge atop the spectacular Grand Mesa.

MUSEUMS

**Museum of Western Colorado**

248 4th Street, (970) 242-0971   www.wcmuseum.org

Great for kids. Features include robotic dinosaurs that spit venom, little plastic baby dinos that hatch from eggs and an experiential imitation earthquake. At the dinosaur hiking trail, the 1.5 mile Trail Through Time, scientists discovered the oldest iguanodon fossil in 1982.

OTHER CLIMBING GUIDES

*Grand Junction Rock: Rock Climbs of Unaweep Canyon and Adjacent Areas* by K.C. Baum, Maury Strahl, Bob Eakle, Chris Becker, Elizabeth Miles, Cris Coffey, 1997.

*Rock Climbing Colorado*, Stewart Green, 1995.

*Colorado Bouldering*, Phillip Benningfield, revised 2006.

*Colorado Bouldering 2*, Phillip Benningfield & Matt Samet, 2003.

**H**

EMERGENCY
INFO
&
MORE

**Community Hospital**
2021 N. 12th St.
(970) 242-0920

**St. Mary's Hospital**
Seventh St. & Patterson Rd.
(970) 244-2273

**Chamber of Commerce**
360 Grand Avenue
(970) 242-3214
www.gjchamber.org

**Mesa County Public Library District**
530 Grand Ave.
(970) 241-5704
Wireless access only at main branch.

**BLM**
Colorado Canyons National Conservation Area
2815 H Road
(970) 244-3000

## SUNDAY WALL

**Warning:**
Cactus spines

**Approach:** From the junction of Divide Road and Highway 141, drive about 2.2 miles west towards Gateway. Park at a pullout beside the road below the Sunday Wall. Climb over the fence on stairs and follow an obvious well-traveled trail uphill to the base of the cliff.
GPS: Elevation – 6,832'          Trailhead: 12 S 0707582 UTH 4299018

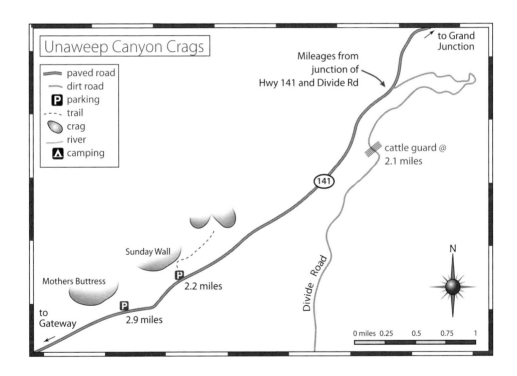

### ____1. Don Juan 5.6 ★★

Follow the trail up from the road until it comes out directly below *Don Juan*. Of the two cracks, the left one is easier. *Don Juan* follows the easier-looking steep finger and hand cracks in a corner to a large ledge. From the ledge, move right and climb up to a second ledge. Rappel from a 2-bolt anchor with rings that is suitable for toproping. 55 ft, small – medium nuts, stoppers, yellow TCU and cams.

GPS: Elevation – 7,839 ft
Climb: 12 S 0707640 UTH 4299316

### ____2. Beginner's Luck 5.7 ★★

From *Don Juan* walk left and up a steep rocky trail for about 200 ft (about 3 – 5 minutes) to a crack beneath an obvious dead tree easily visible from below. At the base, a small flat area with trees provides a shaded belay spot. *Beginner's Luck* follows an obvious right-leaning discontinuous crack to a ledge (about 70 ft). This testy quality route offers insecure jams and reachy moves in a V-groove. Since the crack leans right it's best to leave directionals for toproping. A bolted anchor with D-rings provides a toprope and rappel station.
GPS: Elevation – 7,092 ft
Climb: 12 S 0707612 UTH 4299298

### ____3. Fearless First 5.8

Immediately right of *Beginner's Luck* is *Fearless First*—a stiff and slightly runout 5.8 with bolts and clean gear well below thin insecure face moves. You can traverse to the top from *Beginner's Luck* to toprope it.

### ____4. Bandito 5.8+

About 15 ft right of *Don Juan*, *Bandito* follows a steep, difficult (and hard-to protect) finger crack to the top. The starting moves constitute a boulder problem which feels more like hard 5.9. Once past the strenuous start, the crack becomes enjoyable.

Tristan Hechtel on *Bandito* 5.8+

### 5. Three's Company 5.7+

Uphill and 40 ft to the right of *Bandito*, *Three's Company* goes up a left-facing corner. A finger and hand crack leads to an offwidth that we thought was harder that its 5.7+ rating. (Of course, there is that "+" in the rating!). Rappel from a 2-bolt anchor with rings.

### 6. Sweet Sunday Serenade 5.9 ★★★

*Sweet Sunday Serenade*, while a bit hard and long for a typical family outing, is a worthwhile endeavor if the situation arises. Walk east toward a right-leaning crack in a left-facing corner in an alcove.

**P1.** The first pitch has a hard start for short climbers. A wide stem past a bulge leads to a big jam crack. Shorter climbers will struggle to stem high enough to reach a good jam. The remainder of the route is straightforward and pleasant.

**P2.** The next bit follows finger and hand jams with good pro.

**Descent:** Two rappels lead to a notch with an easy walk-off descent.

GPS: 12 S 0707782 UTH 4299404

**Not Recommended Climbs:**
If referencing another guide in addition to this book, several other moderate routes are here for exploring. These two routes receive a thumbs down.

**Avoid: Standard Route** 5.7. We found the climbing to be fine, but encountered many loose rocks and boulders at the top. It would be dangerous for a leader inexperienced in mountaineering and outdoor climbing with loose rock.

**Avoid: Good One** on the Television Wall. We found routefinding to be difficult and the climbing stiff for the grade.

## Lower Mothers Buttress

From the junction of Divide Road, drive 2.9 miles west towards Gateway. Park at a narrow, ill-defined pullout beside the road below Mothers Buttress. Climb over the barbed wire fence, which is trickier here, sans stairs, and follow an obvious trail uphill to the base of the cliff. The trail emerges at the base of the wall, directly below a large chimney-like alcove some 10 feet across. Several routes, including *Welcoming Party*, are in the back and sides of the alcove.

GPS: Elevation – 6,733 ft        Trailhead: 12 S 0706841 UTH 4298585

 Cactus spines

### 1. Welcoming Party 5.7 ★★

The rightmost crack, *Welcoming Party*, follows a hand crack to a good ledge. From the ledge, the crack widens to form an offwidth and chimney. This is a good place to learn chimney technique and kneepads may prove helpful, as will the suggestion to climb it left side in (where holds can aid progress). The rock in this corridor is coarse enough to warrant taping. Bring cams to a #4 Camalot if you want overhead pro. Be careful of loose blocks and rock at the top of the chimney and don't pull them off onto climbers below.

The two-bolt anchor has no rings, so toprope through quickdraws at the anchor and then all but the last climber can lower. The last person has to descend the backside which is somewhat exposed and requires scrambling and routefinding. I don't recommend taking kids down the descent. By comparison the walk down descent from *Sweet Sunday Serenade* (see previous page) is much easier.

### 2. Unnamed Route 5.9+

The crack five feet left of *Welcoming Party* can be toproped from the same anchor. I recommend placing a directional cam near the top of the crack. Follow the crack up, using finger and hand jams to a bulge. The bulge, which goes from good hand jams to loose insecure finger locks, provides the crux. People who can climb this crack will be happy on *Cow-A-Bunga*.

### 3. Cow-A-Bunga 5.8- ★★

Walk left and slightly uphill to the obvious clean crack near a tree. Follow the crack and chimney for 120 ft to a face with a finger crack. Climb the crack up another 30 ft to a ledge. We found *Cow-a-Bunga* to be the nicest route we climbed at Lower Mothers Buttress. I actually thought it was easier than *Welcoming Party*. For beginners who are insecure in chimneys and offwidths *Cow-a-Bunga* may be a better route to start on.

**Descent:** Descend off the back and to the south, joining the descent for *Welcoming Party*. Standard rack.

Tristan Hechtel on *Welcoming Party* 5.7

Lauren Sigman on 5.7 toprope at Sunset Cantina    Photograph by Sibylle Hechtel

# SAMPLE TRIPS
# SUGGESTIONS BY SEASON

You can climb at various Colorado climbing areas almost any time of the year. Some high-altitude areas enjoy warm summers but wet springs and snowy winters; other lower areas get very hot in summer but allow you to climb during mild spring and fall conditions, and at Shelf Road, you can climb even in December and January. Depending on when you come, you can tour a circuit of several areas that introduces you to a variety of rock and climbing. I've put together some sample trip itineraries for spring or fall areas and for summertime trips. In the spring/fall section, I'll separately discuss gear climbing areas and sport areas.

Colorado weather can change rapidly (one popular saying reads, "If you don't like the weather, wait an hour"). While the areas below are generally best during spring or fall, I've climbed at Eldorado Canyon in December with 68-degree temperatures, and I've been snowed on in June. Check the weather report for the week you plan to travel, and adjust your travel plans accordingly.

## Spring or Fall Climbing Trips

### GEAR AREAS
**Boulder Area** (both gear and sport here)
**South Platte and Elevenmile Canyon**
**Unaweep**

If you're driving here from the east on I-70 or I-80, you can head to Boulder and start your Colorado road trip here. A good place to acclimate to the altitude, you can stock up on climbing gear, outdoor equipment, and camping supplies at Neptune Mountaineering. Near Boulder you can climb at Eldorado Canyon, which features primarily face climbing but has some cracks. Most of the routes here take gear; approaches are generally short. If the weather seems too warm, you can head up to Boulder Canyon and climb at Castle Rock. A bit higher in altitude and located right beside the creek, Castle Rock also faces west so that you can enjoy morning shade.

After getting used to Colorado's generally higher altitude, stock up on food and supplies and head south and west to the South Platte. You can reach the Pine area in about an hour and Turkey Rocks in a little over two hours. These more remote granite areas offer mostly crack climbing with a few friction routes—in a beautiful wild setting. Be sure to take everything you need, since you'll be far from any supermarkets or shopping centers. Bucksnort Slab and Sphinx Rock are closest to Boulder. From here, you can continue south to Turkey Rocks and camp near the climbing. Once you've done a few climbs at Turkey Rocks, it's a relatively short drive south to Elevenmile Canyon. The granite here is somewhat smoother (or at least less rough) than that of Turkey Rocks. You'll find both slab and crack climbs here, plus gorgeous and well-equipped campsites.

From Elevenmile Canyon, you can head west toward Buena Vista, over Fremont Pass near Leadville to I-70, and west toward Grand Junction and Unaweep Canyon. Generally Unaweep is warmer than the South Platte area, so if it's a cool spring, you can escape to warmer and dryer climbing. Unaweep consists primarily of crack climbing, ranging from finger and hand cracks to chimneys. If you've honed your crack technique in the South Platte, you'll be ready for the cracks here.

**SPORT AREAS**
**Castlewood Canyon**
**Shelf Road**
**Penitente Canyon**

If you feel unsure of your gear-placing abilities, or simply prefer clipping bolts, you can choose among several sport areas in spring or fall.

Castlewood Canyon, south of Denver, offers quie a few short cliffs with numerous lines. Head south from here to Shelf Road, where camping on BLM land provides a peaceful experience.

Shelf Road, near Cañon City, will be driest and warmest, since it sits at the lowest altitude and at least half of the crags face directly south. I've climbed here in shorts over Thanksgiving and in January. However, nights get quite cold and long in fall, even after warm days.

From Shelf Road, you can head south on SH 285 to Penitente, which also provides spacious, quiet sites on BLM land. The crags here line both sides of a canyon, so you can choose whether to climb in the sun or in the shade. A little higher in altitude than Shelf Road, Penitente may feature slightly cooler temperatures.

**Summer Trips**

**Vedauwoo**
**Estes Park**
**South Platte and Elevenmile**
**Independence Pass**

I'd consider two of these areas primarily summer areas – Vedauwoo and Independence Pass. I've camped at Independence Pass over the July 4th weekend and woken up with frost on the windshield. And luckily I missed this particular weekend at Vedauwoo, but the campground host reported that in early June it snowed 14 inches.

If you have a week or two to travel around Colorado in summer, I'd start with Vedauwoo (yes, it's in Wyoming, but barely over the border!). Vedauwoo embraces beautiful scenery, great camping, and numerous easy climbs—both crack and face. Vedauwoo sits at a lower altitude than both Estes Park and Independence Pass and most climbs have short approaches, letting you ease into climbing for Colorado's higher altitudes. Spend a few days here, getting accustomed to crack climbing, altitude, and the dry air before heading up even higher.

From Vedauwoo, head south into Colorado and up to Estes Park, a good warm day destination in late spring or early fall. You can choose between climbing at Jurassic Park near Lily Lake (primarily a bolted sport climbing area) or at Lumpy Ridge, on slightly larger cliffs with mostly gear routes. Both areas will require a longer approach than Vedauwoo—about a half hour to Jurassic Park, and close to 45 minutes to reach Lumpy Ridge.

If you're not quite ready to face both long hikes as well as multi-pitch climbs at high altitude, head from Vedauwoo down to the South Platte for a few days. You can choose between very short (five minutes) approaches or slightly longer ones (about 20 minutes) to short, one-pitch climbs at a lower altitude than Estes Park. After a bit more time acclimatizing, and developing your crack technique, you can then choose to head up to Estes Park, or if it's really hot, spend a few days at Independence Pass.

Independence Pass, at around 10,000 feet, enjoys the coolest days. Approaches are luckily short and the area provides many one-pitch climbs, mostly bolted sport routes. I think it's some of the most beautiful scenery with great campgrounds, so don't miss this area.

## Winter Trips

### Shelf Road
### Boulder Area
### Castlewood Canyon

This is Colorado, the country's ski capital...
*so when in Rome.* That said, while you may not
plan a family trip here to climb in the winter, if
you end up here on a business trip and want to
climb, there are options for climbing in winter.
Shelf Road is primarily a winter area, being the
lowest altitude area of the places described as
well as possessing south-facing terrain.

Castlewood Canyon also gets good sun and is
close to Denver, if you have business there.

It's possible to climb in Eldorado Canyon in
winter, as long as you pick a sunny day and a
climb in the sun. The canyon goes into the sun
late in the day and loses it early, so plan on a
short climbing day.

Boulder Canyon lies a bit higher and gets less
sun, so you may be better off heading for Eldorado Canyon. Table Mountain, near Golden,
one of the areas I mention in *Other Areas* also
receives lots of winter sun, so you could try
climbing here if you end up near Boulder
in winter.

# SAMPLE DAYS

For a few areas, I give a *Sample Day* description. I describe this specifically at Unaweep, where one of its two main beginner areas is much better. If you're there for only a day you may as well go to the better cliff. For Shelf Road, I describe a *Sample Day* itinerary, since you can choose a selection of climbs and try them all in one or two days.

Some areas don't require a *Sample Day* itinerary, since you can climb all the routes I include in one or two days and they're all good climbs. Penitente is compact enough that you can walk past the base, see all the climbs, and choose the ones you like. Other areas, like Estes Park, offer several options that are all great and come down to individual preference. At Estes Park, you can choose between gear climbing or sport climbing, and with gear climbs you can choose one of several crags. Here, the choice depends more on your specific climbing interests.

## Shelf Road Cactus Cliff: Sample Day

Head up to the new parking for Cactus Cliff at The Bank, and hike about 35 minutes to the trailhead which begins at the former parking lot. Walk about five minutes to *Alexi's Climb*.

Eight stone steps lead up to a flat base area. A rock buttress on the right borders the edge of the alcove. A few pine trees below the trail provide a good place to tie up your dog or hang up your sleeping baby in her baby carrier.

Here, children and beginners can enjoy two easy routes. *Alexi's Climb* (5.5) offers closely-spaced bolts topped by a large, flat ledge beside the anchor for the beginning leader. For children who've climbed in the gym, but are new to the outdoors, this could be a great first climb on real rock. It's relatively low-angle and well pro-tected with lots of big holds. If your kids have led climbs in the gym, and are used to following routes outdoors on limestone, this can be a great first lead for your new leader.

From the ledge at the top of *Alexi's Climb*, I taught my son how to rappel and how to feed the rope through the anchors. Tristan led the climb and then belayed me up to the ledge. While I watched closely, he fed the rope through

the anchor rings and set up the rappel. Teaching kids to thread the anchor is much easier and safer for both parent and child if there's a nice, spacious ledge for both to stand on while learning to do this correctly.

Just right of *Alexi's Climb*, you can do *Ian's Climb* and either use the same anchor, or the anchor to the right.

Further right, *Amiga*, a layback and arête, goes at 5.10b. Around the corner to the right (another five steps) *Ol'Four-Seven* (5.9) offers your third route in the alcove, topping out on a large flat ledge. Beware of rockfall here, and keep kids well back from the cliff, due to loose rocks on the ledge.

If your friends or family have climbed all three routes here, and want to climb more, a short walk will get you to another easy route. About 50 steps to the right of this cluster, you'll find *Oscar de la Cholla*, a two-star 5.9-. Two parallel cracks about halfway up distinguish this crack from its neighbors. With seven bolts in 75 feet, some climbers have complained that the lower crack section is a bit run out.

## Shelf Road Cactus Cliff: Sample Day

After a two-minute walk to the right you'll reach *Lacholla Jackson*, a four-star 5.8 and my son's first lead at Shelf. Cholla (rhymes with LaToya) are the abundant cacti growing everywhere.

Don't miss this climb—it's worth every one of its four stars.

After all these climbs, Tristan usually says, "Can we go to Alfonso's Supertaco now?"

View from Sunday Wall

## Unaweep: Sample Day

Head to the Sunday Wall.

The trail comes out at the base of the cliff right next to *Don Juan*, a straightforward 5.6 crack. If your kids or older relatives are new to crack climbing, this can be a good introduction to chimneys and stemming. If you want to teach your family to rappel, the ledge is large and comfortable enough that you can belay them up to you from the anchor, and then supervise while they set up their rappel system. Rappelling down can be a little tricky if they stay in the chimney. It's easier to toss the rope off to the right, by *Bandito*.

Once they've mastered chimneys and rappelling, if anyone says it was too easy, put them on a toprope on *Bandito*. This finger crack, with its hard start, should give most of your party something to work on.

From here, hike left and uphill to *Beginner's Luck*. Again, the start is a bit reachy, but once you get in the crack the rest of this route is as easy as *Don Juan*. A low-angle crack and face leads up to another nice ledge with good anchors.

The insatiable climbers in your group can toprope *Fearless First* from *Beginner's Luck* and

toprope this climb. We found this fairly hard for a 5.8, so expect some struggles.

By now, the wall should be going in the sun and it can get quite hot up here. After four pitches, everyone may be ready for a break. We drove down the canyon to the creek on the drive to Whitewater. Numerous pulloffs let you drive down toward the creek and park in the shade. We enjoyed a pleasant picnic here and soaked our feet in the creek.

After a relaxing break, you can drive up the road to one of the numerous bouldering areas lining both sides of Hwy 141 for an afternoon bouldering session. We liked the Fossil Boulder because it's right next to the parking and it has an easy route that gets shade in the afternoon. Bouldering here should tire out anyone that still has an overabundance of energy after the morning's climbs.

From here, it's a short drive to the campground, where the kids can go collect wood and build a campfire. Across Divide Road, a dirt road leads up to a flagstone collecting area. The rock is unremarkable, but there is a nice view of the Grand Mesa and you can admire the sunset from here.

# OTHER AREAS
## WHY ISN'T XXX AREA IN THE BOOK?

What about the many other great climbing areas in Colorado, like Rifle or the Black Canyon? Why aren't they included in this book? Should you go? I'll briefly describe other good areas that I've omitted from this book. Some areas have none, or very few, easy routes; or they may have long or exposed approaches and descents.

### Clear Creek Canyon near Golden

This area was originally covered in the guide. Cat Slab and Highwire have numerous pleasant climbs from 5.4 to 5.9 and wonderful amenities and activities abound in the area. However, the access at Cat Slab could be forever closed, and the fall potential along the hike to Highwire isn't suitable for children. There have been serious injuries and a death along the hike. Traffic and noise add to a feeling of unease. With kids along, any element that heightens anxiety is a major drawback.

### Black Canyon of the Gunnison

Spectacular climbs on dramatic rock abound here, but they're hard, scary, and serious. However, they're not quite as desperate and committing as they were some years ago. The descent gullies to the climbs now have signs telling you where they start, with a fairly easy trail down to the base of the routes.

A resident climbing ranger, Brent Mims, is more than happy to draw you a topo and provide accurate and current route information. If you stick to the easier classics, you should have an enjoyable climbing experience. Still, the climbs are long, with a long, committing approach. The ever-present possibility of afternoon thunderstorms lends a certain urgency to the climbs. You want to get to the base at first light. Our first two climbs here, *Escape Artist* and *Comic Relief*, were excellent climbs on generally good

rock with reasonable route finding. Still, I've heard many horror stories of loose rock, huge runouts, rotten pegmatite, and route-finding problems from enough climbers to have the utmost respect for the harder, more serious routes here.

If you want to climb here, and only bring the family along to visit, the campground at the North Rim is very pleasant. The well-spaced shadey sites have water from a pump, picnic tables, and vault toilets. Your friends can enjoy the spectacular panorama or drive to nearby lakes to relax.

*Black Canyon Rock Climbs*, Robbie Williams

### Buena Vista Crags

I debated whether to include this area, but feel that it's not really a destination area or worth coming to primarily for the climbing. Buena Vista, sometimes called *Colorado's Whitewater Capital*, has great rafting, beautiful scenery, and lies amidst terrific hiking and other outdoor activities. While you can climb here, it's not necessarily worth planning a trip for a climbing vacation.

### Garden of the Gods in Colorado Springs

While there are some easy climbs, I didn't feel that this outweighs the drawbacks of this area. You're in the middle of a city with no nearby camping, the rock is fairly loose, and compared with some other places you could climb, the number of quality routes probably doesn't merit a trip.

### Table Mountain in Golden

Loved and reviled by climbers in the Boulder-Denver metro area, Table Mountain has its adherents. However, the approach is uphill and somewhat long for grandma, most climbs are fairly stout, and the scenery (an eagle-eye view of the Coors Beer factory) can't compete with

Rocky Mountain National Park. Plus, you not only see the factory, but from the cliff you can also hear and smell it. The routes are short and the movement isn't really that pleasant. If you end up near Golden on a business trip in winter, and it's too cold to climb anywhere else, you could visit this cliff. I can't recommend making a special trip to climb here.

## Greyrock, Fort Collins

With a stiff one hour approach (which would translate easily into one and a half hours with kids), I can't recommend this rock for a family outing.

## Rifle

Rifle, without a doubt, has world-class climbing and attracts many international visitors. If you can do the climbs here, you don't need this book! My sport-climbing friends tell me that the 5.11s are greasy, and the climbing only gets good on the 5.12s and 5.13s. This places the climbing well beyond the scope of my book.

## San Juans and Ouray

Often called "The Little Switzerland of America" Ouray has splendid scenery, wonderful mountains, and the famous Ouray Ice Park, home of the famous Ouray Ice Festival. If you want to try ice climbing, Ouray is probably the best place to start.

While some shorter or easier routes exist, most climbs are harder, longer or further away and thus beyond the scope of this book. If you want to visit this area, the guide school below can help you.

San Juan Mountain Guides
(970) 325-4925
www.ourayclimbing.com

## Colorado National Monument

One of the easiest climbs here (*Otto's Route*, 5.8+) has four pitches and you descend by doing three double-rope rappels. While I've included technically harder climbs in the book, they're easier to escape from if anyone has difficulties on the climb.

# EARLY CLIMBING TRIPS
# WITH TRISTAN

One of my friends asked to hear more about my experiences traveling and climbing with my son when he was little. Our very first climb, with Tristan along, was when he was two and a half months old. It was my birthday, and a glorious, warm sunny day in February. When asked what I wanted for my birthday, I said, "I want to go climbing." So we did. A friend carried Tristan in a baby carrier and we headed to Eldorado's West Ridge (note that I did not include this in my list of child-friendly climbs, due to the tricky approach). Hiking in on the trail wasn't bad, until we came to the obstacle rock. We climbed up one at a time, handed the baby and his backpack up and down the cliff, and scrambled down the other side of the rock. Finally we reached the cliff. Our friend sat on a flat rock with Tristan; I scrambled up easy third-class terrain to the base, and started belaying and Tristan got hungry! He wouldn't stop crying.

"I've got to go down and nurse him!" I yelled. I tied off the rope to a tree, Greg tied himself off to a few nuts in the middle of the pitch, and I scrambled back down. After feeding Tristan, I scrambled back up to the ledge, untied my partner from the tree, and put him back on belay. The rest of the climbs proceeded uneventfully.

I'd recommend that if you're climbing with small infants that are still nursing, it's better to choose routes that start on the ground with a good belay spot near the base. Also, if you're with a third person, it may be better for them to belay the leader so that Mom can nurse the baby until she's ready to climb.

## First Vacation
When Tristan was 7 months old, we went to Devil's Tower, Wyoming. We hired a nanny to watch Tristan while we climbed. Devil's Tower

has a flat grassy campground with a paved path good for strollers, a playground with sand and swings, and another paved path around the Tower. Our nanny took walks with Tristan while we climbed a few pitches in the morning, came back to eat and feed the baby (still nursing hungrily), and went back up for a few more pitches in the afternoon.

On one route, we ran into my friends Annie Whitehouse and the late Derek Hersey, the famous British soloist. We were in the middle of a multi-pitch climb and I told Annie that I had to go back down to camp. When Derek asked why we had to descend instead of finishing our route, I replied that I had to nurse my baby. "Why?" he asked. "Can't your nanny nurse the baby?"

After laughing hysterically, we explained the American usage of 'nursing' (not the British usage, should you climb abroad). Annie, an Everest veteran then told us of the Nepali women she's met who left the babies in the village with other moms, and how any woman would nurse any other woman's baby. This makes good sense —a mother of a one-year old can go back out to work, while the mothers of younger infants watch and feed the babies.

## Second Road Trip
When Tristan was nine months old, we got ambitious and met my parents in Yosemite. My mother wisely decided that she'd rent a tent cabin, which had nearby showers and our own picnic table. We climbed with my Dad while my mother played with her grandson. All went well, thanks to my mother's foresight in renting a tent cabin, as getting a campsite in Yosemite in summer varies from difficult to impossible.

Driving back, we stopped at City of Rocks. With only the 2 of us, we carried Tristan to the base in his backpack. Luckily, he always was and still is a good sleeper (he inherited that from me). He was sound asleep once we reached the base, so we hung the baby carrier up in a tree next to the climb with several slings. While the baby slept soundly, we got in several pitches of climbing.

## First Trip Abroad

When Tristan was three years old, I went on the Austrian Women's Shishapangma Expedition in Tibet. My plane ticket allowed me a stopover in Germany, so I met Tristan and Greg near Munich. Here we hooked up with a German climber, Michi Olzowy, who drove to Arco, Italy, with us. Tristan developed several hobbies here: collecting snails (live), snail shells, and pretty rocks. Germany, with all the rain, has a vast amount of beautiful snails with multicolored striped shells. He'd collect the snails and keep them in a large potted plant near the door and feed them leftover lettuce. My aunt, whose main objective had always been to eradicate as many snails as possible viewed this askance. At age three, he could walk to most of the climbs in Arco, with their short approaches, and then collect either snails or rocks near the base.

From Arco, we drove to Finale Ligure on the Mediterranean coast. This became Tristan's favorite climbing area until age 14, when we climbed at the Costa Daurada in Spain. Finale has great ice cream stands everywhere, awesome food, and tons of easy short climbs on limestone with short approaches. It's six kilometers from the beach, so you can climb in the morning and go to the beach in the afternoon.

## First Hard Lead

When Tristan was 10, he and I went alone to Finale Ligure, Italy. This sounds like it should work well—but I had my broken wrist in a cast. Since we already booked our flights, and the cast was due off in another week, we went anyway. One day in Arco, as we walked up to the easy climbs, we encountered two German women having trouble.

"Can you help us?" one asked. "We tried this route which we think is a 4 and can't get up." One of the women had led the first part of a climb, clipping the first four bolts by climbing partly in the chimney next to the route and reaching over to clip. Once the crack ended, and the route forced her onto the face, she couldn't continue.

"It's our first time ever climbing by ourselves without our husbands," the other told me. "We borrowed their guidebook to try to climb on our own. We don't want to ask them for a rescue." After years of promoting women's climbing, I supported that view entirely.

We looked at their guidebook and I soon realized that not only couldn't they lead, but they also couldn't read a guidebook description. The 4 about a 5.5 or 5.6, easily within their capabilities, was far away They'd blundered onto a 6a+ (about 5.10a or b). I'd led some 5s, but didn't think I could climb a thin finger crack with a cast. I could lead easy routes by using the ring and little finger of my right hand (in a cast), but the other fingers were immobilized and the cast prevented me from moving my thumb to clip the rope. I had to climb a route easy enough to hold on with the little finger and then clip with my good left hand.

"I'll lead it!" Tristan volunteered.

"Do you think you can?" I asked. He'd started leading that year, but only 5.8s.

"I can try," he enthusiastically replied.

I could see that the job of rescuing two women appealed to him. We belayed him up to the fourth bolt, the last the leader had clipped before descending. He tried the next few moves, struggled, and came back to rest on the bolt.

"I don't know if I can do this," he said. No wonder. It was April; we hadn't climbed much since last year, when he was nine years old and not leading. He had little leading experience and nothing nearly this difficult.

"I'll try," I volunteered. As expected, I couldn't do the moves with the thin finger crack, with most of my hand in a cast. I came back down and we looked at one another.

"I'll do it," Tristan said. He went back up, got to the bolt, rested, shook out, tried the moves a few times, and got up to the next bolt. After

a bit more struggling, he got up the climb. The 2 women praised him and offered him treats. I said I'd buy him a gelato (yummy Italian ice cream) when we got back to town.

Once back in town, sitting in the town square enjoying his gelato, he asked, "Can I have an ice cream for every climb I lead?"

"If it's a hard enough route," I replied, not wanting to break my budget on Italian gelatos.

"How hard?" he persevered.

We settled on 6a, about 5.10a. After that deal, he'd grab the guidebook for every cliff we reached, both in Arco and Finale, and look for 6a's that he liked and thought he could lead. By the end of the trip, I'd trained myself a good rope gun for the cost of a daily ice cream.

# ABOUT THE AUTHOR

Sibylle Hechtel started mountain climbing with her father, Richard Hechtel, in her native Germany at about age three. After they immigrated to the United States, she started hanging out in Camp 4 with her mother and grandmother while her father got stuck on unplanned bivies high on Yosemite's big walls. In her teens, she started climbing in Yosemite with her dad, which resulted in fewer unexpected bivouacs. At 17, once she went to college, she expanded her range of climbing partners with the consequence of being exposed to a number of unplanned bivouacs of her own. She's writing this book in part to save other kids and parents from these dire consequences.

Sibylle and Beverly Johnson made the first all-female ascent of Yosemite's El Capitan via the *Triple Direct*, or *Integral*, route. Sibylle then went on to do the first female unguided ascent of the *Salathe Wall* (Royal Robbins guided a married couple up this route, so he got, in addition to the second ascent of El Cap, also the first female ascent of the Salathe). After this, she did make the first female clean El Cap ascent, of the Nose in 1977 (before the invention of camming devices.)

She ventured into alpine climbing with trips to Canada's Rockies, to Ak-Su in Kyrgyzstan, Everest, and Shishapangma, but gave this up after several of her climbing partners died. She now climbs all over North America and Europe with her son whenever she can get him out of school.

| Sharp End Book Titles | Price |
|---|---|
| Betty and the Silver Spider: Welcome to Gym Climbing (Instructional) | $12.95 |
| Black Canyon Rock Climbs (CO) | $28.00 |
| A Bouldering Guide to Utah | $34.95 |
| Castles in the Sand: A Climber's Guide to Sedona and Oak Creek Canyon (AZ) | $24.95 |
| Central Washington Bouldering: Leavenworth and Goldbar | $25.00 |
| Classic Boulder Climbs (CO) | $9.95 |
| Classic Desert Climbs, 3rd Edition (UT, CO) | $15.95 |
| Clear Creek Canyon Rock Climbs (CO) | $28.00 |
| Colorado Bouldering (The Original) | $29.93 |
| Colorado Bouldering 2 (New Developed Areas and Problems) | $28.00 |
| Climbing Free: My Life in a Vertical World Lynn Hill ( Hard/Soft Cover-Autographed!) | $24.95/$15.95 |
| Double Down: A Select Guide to Vegas Limestone and Sandstone (NV) | $14.00 |
| Enchanted Rock: A Climber's Guide (TX) | $16.95 |
| Front Range Topropes (CO) | $16.95 |
| Fun Climbs Colorado: Best Family Climbing Vacations | $22.00 |
| A Guide to Rock Climbing in Northern Thailand | $24.95 |
| Gunnison Rock | $32.95 |
| Indian Creek: A Climbing Guide (UT) **Full Color** | $32.95 |
| Jemez Rock and Pecos Area (NM) | $28.00 |
| Life by the Drop: Ice and Mixed Climbs Surrounding CO's San Luis Valley | $14.00 |
| Long Dong Trad Climbs (Taiwan) | $28.00 |
| Mountain Biking Colorado's Western Slope (CO) | $9.95 |
| New River Gorge: Meadow River and Summersville Lake Climbing Guide (WV) | $29.95 |
| Northern Utah Limestone | $16.95 |
| Ogden Area Climbing Guide: From Brigham City to Echo Canyon (UT) | $19.95 |
| Oklahoma Select: A Climber's Guide | $16.95 |
| The Park: Climbs of Rocky Mountain National Park (CO) | $9.95 |
| Red Rock Canyon Open Space (CO) | $9.95 |
| Rifle: Climbers' Guide to Rifle Mountain Park (CO) | $7.95 |
| The Ripper: Rock, Ice and Bouldering in the Wet Mountains near Pueblo, CO | $14.00 |
| Rock Climbs of Southwest Utah and the Arizona Strip, 2nd Edition **Full Color** | $32.95 |
| The Rock Warrior's Way (Instructional Book or Audio Book on CD) | $18.95/$29.95 |
| Sandia Rock (NM) | $14.95 |
| Serious Play: An Annotated Guide to Front Range Trad Classics 5.2-5.9 (CO) | $18.00 |
| Shelf Road Rock: The Complete Climbing Reference (CO) | $28.00 |
| South Platte Rock (CO) | $12.95 |
| Spearfish Canyon Limestone (SD) | $14.95 |
| Taos Rock (NM) | $19.95 |
| Tuolumne Topropes (CA) | $10.95 |
| Winter Trails of the Front Range (CO, Snowshoe and XC Ski) | $7.95 |
| Yosemite Topropes (CA) | $8.95 |
| Zion Canyoneering (UT) | $19.95 |
| Zion Rock (UT) | $14.00 |
| **Video Titles** | |
| Australia Project (DVD - New Title) | $30.00 |
| Comfortably Numb (DVD) | $29.95 |
| A Day in the Life: 5 Women Who Climb (DVD) | $24.95 |
| First Ascent (New Title, You Will LOVE it.) | $30.00 |
| Fitlife Pilates (VHS) | $15.00 |
| Friction Addiction (VHS and DVD) | $30.00 |
| Free Climbing the Nose (Lynn Hill, VHS) | $14.95 |
| Front Range Freaks (VHS and DVD) | $30.00 |
| Inertia 1 & 2 (DVD) | $24.95 |
| Just Tie It (Instructional, DVD) | $12.95 |
| Karma (DVD) | $30.00 |
| King Lines | $29.95 |
| Red River Ruckus (DVD) | $29.95 |
| Return2Sender (DVD) | $30.00 |
| Soul Cal (DVD) | $29.98 |
| Spray | $29.95 |
| Yoga for Climbers (DVD) | $22.95 |